INSIGHTS ON DOMESTIC STAKEHOLDERS AND CLIMATE ACTION:

Issues, Social Forces, and Dynamics of Compliance with the UNFCCC in a Developing Country

ZAKARI ZIRRA

CB

ISBN:
978-1-952874-32-1 (paperback)
978-1-952874-33-8 (hardback)
978-1-952874-34-5 (ebook)

Published by:

OMNIBOOK CO.
99 Wall Street, Suite 118
New York, NY 10005
USA
+1-866-216-9965
www.omnibookcompany.com

First Edition

For e-book purchase: Kindle on Amazon, Barnes and Noble
Book purchase: Amazon.com, Barnes & Noble,
and www.omnibookcompany.com

Omnibook titles may be purchased in bulk for educational, business,
fund-raising, or sales promotional use. For more information
please e-mail info@omnibookcompany.com

DEDICATION

I dedicate this work to all climate action advocates
whose unflinching tenacity remains nature's last defence
and hope for sustainability.

PREFACE

Years ago, while researching for an article on climate governance in Nigeria ahead of the Paris Agreement of 2015, I realized the near absence of indigenous international relations texts on the subject. Rather, climate governance was overshadowed by the general scientific plot on the environment. Indeed, all the experts I was referred to, were climate scientists, one of whom advised that I should approach a political scientist for guidance on the governance of the subject.

Unknown to me, this advice was the start of a daunting adventure, the cusp of which led to my realization that; if progress must be achieved in a strategic manner on climate change, the subject must be mainstreamed into governance studies. This was my catharsis. Climate governance cannot be orphaned in general policy discourse in Nigeria, whilst the climate emergency is already upon us. Not at a time when scholars of power are shaping the global narrative on the subject in other climes. As we shall see, it is the "politics" in the global power dynamics that slows climate action and not the "science." Hence, we need to build a robust governance architecture that can successfully coordinate the various climate action initiatives. This is crucial for any meaningful progress in any of the sustainable development goals; especially now that we have entered the decade of action.

Against this background, I proceeded to specialise in climate change for my doctoral studies. I embarked on this book project afterwards, combining materials from my thesis and other library sources. I thank all the respondents and interviewees whose feedback assisted greatly in framing my doctoral thesis. This book copiously benefits from your rich perspectives therein. I wrote this book with the objective of helping post-graduate students and professionals involved in Nigeria's climate governance. Dr. Usman Abuh Tom of Nasarawa State University deserves a special place for taking me under his wings in this voyage of discovery. Sadly, he passed on before the first print hit the stable. May his soul find peace with God. This prognosis exposes the key stakeholders and what they have done as social forces to drive climate action in the country in line with the United Nations Framework Convention on Climate Change (UNFCCC). The book contains some detailed information about where Nigeria stands in her gas flaring emission inventory and mitigation initiatives. Some of these the reader will not find in any other standard text. The book goes on to stimulate debate on Nigeria's compliance with the UNFCCC. These are quite useful as we strive to achieve the Sustainable Development Goals and the terms of the Paris Agreement. Hence, unlike my experience at the beginning of the study, today anybody interested in understanding the dynamics of climate governance in Nigeria can recourse to this book as a guide.

Finally, in writing this book, materials from natural sciences, law, social sciences and the arts were synthesized from both local and foreign sources. Consequently, my plain writing style also takes into consideration, professionals from these diverse disciplines. I render gratitude to all the authors who have been duly attributed for their body of work. And for any content that is not properly attributed, expeditious rectification will be effected as soon as such is brought to my attention. In this connection, I specially thank Prof. Asisi Asobie, Prof. Bulus Gadiga and Dr. Atta Barkindo for their guidance in my academic pursuit. This work would not be possible without access to academic materials in the repositories of the Nigerian Institute of International Affairs Lagos and the Nasarawa State University Keffi. You all deserve credit for your contributions to climate governance scholarship. I am confident this will be a great resource in the emerging corpus on climate governance in Nigeria.

In all things may God be praised.

Zakari Zirra

TABLE OF CONTENTS

CHAPTER 1 — 1
OVERVIEW

CHAPTER TWO — 7
CONCEPTUALISING CLIMATE GOVERNANCE

CHAPTER THREE — 27
NIGERIA AND THE UNFCCC AGREEMENTS

LIST OF TABLES

LIST OF FIGURES

LIST OF APPENDICES

LIST OF ABBREVIATIONS

AAP	Africa Adaptation Programme
ADC	Advanced Developing Countries
AfDB	African Development Bank
AOSIS	Association of Small Island States
AU	African Union
AWG	Ad Hoc Working Group
AWG-LCA	Ad-Hoc Working Group- Long-Term Cooperative Action
BRIC	Brazil, Russia, India and China
BNRCC	Building Nigeria's Response to Climate Change
CBD	Convention on Biological Biodiversity
CBDR	Common But Differentiated Responsibilities
CDM	Clean Development Mechanism
CMP	Conference of Meeting on the Protocol
CEIT	Country with Economy in Transition
CER	Certified Emissions Reduction
CH_4	Methane
CO_2	Carbon Dioxide
COP	Conference of the Parties
CSO	Civil Society Organisations
CTCN	Climate Technology Centre and Network
DC	Developed Country
DFID	Department for International Development
DNA	Designated National Authority
EC	Economic Commission

ECN	Energy Commission of Nigeria
ECOWAS	Economic Community of West African States
EGTT	Expert Group on Technology Transfer
EPA	Environmental Protection Agency
ERGP	Economic Recovery and Growth Plan
ETS	Emissions Trading Scheme
EU	European Union
FDI	Foreign Direct Investment
FGN	Federal Government of Nigeria
FMEnv	Federal Ministry of Environment
FNC	First National Communication
G-77	Group of 77 Nations
GCF	Green Climate Fund
GDP	Gross Domestic Product
GEF	Global Environment Facility
GGW	Great Green Wall
GHG	Greenhouse Gas
GWP	Global Warming Potential
HDI	Human Development Index
HFCs	Hydro Fluorocarbons
ICAO	International Civil Aviation Organisation
ICJ	International Court of Justice
IDRC	International Development Research Centre
IGO	Inter-Governmental Organisation
IPCC	Intergovernmental Panel on Climate Change
KP	Kyoto Protocol
LACs	Latin American Countries

LDC	Least Developed Countries
LDCF	Least Developed Countries Fund
LDCs	Least Developed Countries
LEG	LDC Expert Group
LULUCF	Land Use, Land Use Change and Forestry
MDGs	Millennium Development Goals
MEAs	Multilateral Environmental Agreements
MRV	Monitoring, Reporting and Verification
MTOe	Million Tonnes of Oil Equivalent
N_2O	Nitrous Oxide
NAMAs	Nationally Appropriate Mitigation Actions
NAPA	National Adaptation Programmes of Action
NASA	National Aeronautic and Space Agency
NASPA	National Adaptation Strategy and Plan of Action
NC	National Communication
NCCR	Nigeria Climate Change Roundtable
NCP	Non-Compliance Procedure
NDC	Nationally Determined Contribution
NEPAD	New Partnership for Africa's Development
NESREA	Nigeria Environmental Standards, Regulation and Enforcement Agency
NGO	Non-Governmental Organisation
NGOs	Non-Governmental Organizations
NiMET	Nigeria Meteorological Agency
NNPC	Nigeria National Petroleum Corporation
NEEAP	National Energy Efficiency Action Plan
NREP	National Renewable Energy Action Plan

O3	Ozone
OCHA	Office of the Coordinator of Humanitarian Affairs
ODA	Official Development Assistance
OECD	Organization of Economic Cooperation and
OPEC	Organisation for Petroleum Exporting Countries
PFCs	Perfluorocarbons
REDD	Reduced Emissions from Deforestation and Forest
REEEP	Renewable Energy and Energy Efficiency Policy
SBI	Subsidiary Body for Implementation
SBSTA	Subsidiary Body for Scientific and Technological
SCCF	Special Climate Change Fund
SF6	Sulphur Hexafluoride
ShE	Stakeholders in Environment
SIDS	Small Island Developing States
SNC	Second National Communication
TNC	Third National Communication
UNDP	United Nations Development Programme
UNDRIP	United Nations Declaration on the Rights of Indigenous Peoples
UNECA	United Nations Economic Commission for Africa
UNEP	United Nations Environment Programme
UNFCCC	United Nations Framework Convention on Climate Change
UNGA	United Nations General Assembly
UNIDO	United Nations Industrial Development Organization
WWF	World Wide Fund for Nature

CHAPTER 1

OVERVIEW

█ INTRODUCTION

Since the United Nations' Rio Convention of 1992, the issue of climate change has taken centre stage in international relations. Significant carbon related emissions (Greenhouse Gases-GHG) from human endeavours which affected the atmosphere and threatened life systems started raising apprehensions about a possible tipping point.

Following the Rio Convention, the United Nations Framework Convention on Climate Change was established as the globally accepted benchmark for regulating climate change by state parties. The agreements outline the roles of developed as well as developing countries in ensuring the reduction of GHG and the conservation of the environment to save the planet. So far, 197 parties have signed the UNFCCC; showing a near universal concurrence that there is a problem requiring action (Ngoweh, 2016). The agreements encourage all parties to take action on two fronts - Mitigation and Adaptation (UNFCCC, 2014).

Unfortunately, despite signed agreements by all parties, a lot of countries have failed in complying. While developed nations are urged under the framework to show leadership by reducing GHG emissions, things have basically remained the same. Developing countries too are being faulted for being responsible for more GHG emissions most especially since the turn of the millenium. The accusation and counter accusation of non-compliance with the framework has resulted in stalemate under the framework. In reaction to this sad development, Dauvergne in a ground-breaking study on climate change governance submits that "unless strict restraints are put in place, humans will exhaust the globe's natural resources, fill its sinks and overstep the earth's capacity to support life" (Dauvergne, 2004, p. 373). In the meantime, the impact of climate change continues to worsen with developing countries suffering the most vulnerable impact.

Figure 1.1 Map of Nigeria and her neighbours.

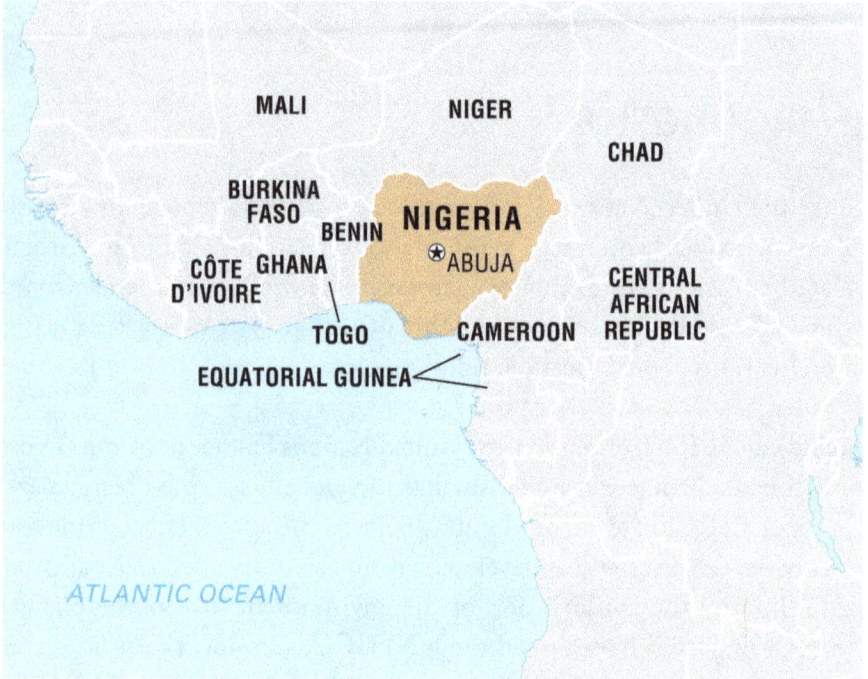

Source: Adapted from Encyclopaedia Brittanica 2020.

As a developing country, Nigeria is affected by whatever concerns that relate to countries in this category. Given the focus of this text on Nigeria, it is necessary to provide a concise profile of the country.

Nigeria has a land mass of 923 768 km². She is located in West Africa with a coastline of 853 Km along the southern margins of the country. Nigeria is the most populated country in Africa with an increasing population of 203,707,940 (two hundred and three million, seven hundred and seven thousand, nine hundred and forty). There are five geographical zones: in the north are the low plateau and the high plateau zones. In the south lie the coastal zone by the Gulf of Guinea and the mountainous eastern borders with the country's highest elevation called chappal waddi. In the middle of the country is the river valley zone from the Benue and Niger rivers (Nkeki, Henah & Nduka, 2013). These divergent topography exposes her to the negative effects of climate variability. Her weather is a combination of varying degrees of cool and warm winds in the south, in contrast to dry and mostly hot periods in the north with varying levels of rainfall which have left the country with varying degrees of environmental degradation attributed to climate change.

Nigeria's resources which include petroleum, tin, columbite, iron ore, coal, limestone, lead, zinc, natural gas, hydropower and arable land place her at a critical position as an active player in climate change. The petroleum industry is the largest industry in Nigeria and is the main generator of Gross Domestic Product (GDP) and foreign exchange. Fishing, farming and cattle rearing constitute the main occupation of most of a large part of the populace. With climate change, the environmental condition for these activities to continue is endangered, hence undermining sustainable development efforts in different spheres. Meanwhile as a signatory to the UNFCCC, Nigeria has voluntary obligation to mitigate the effects of and adapt to climate change.

With her high dependence on fossil fuel, proximity to the high sea and Sahel region, the impact of climate change is identified as a clear and present danger. Annually, the country's National Emergency Management Agency releases statistics of persons rendered homeless because of flooding in all parts of the country. Rise in atmospheric temperature has also been recorded in all parts of the country. In other words, the devastating impact of climate change in Nigeria makes it imperative for the country to act. Moreover, as a signatory to the UNFCCC the onus is on Nigeria to take action to prevent or reduce the impact of climate change. This calls for a robust discourse on the key actors or stakeholders in the country's climate change scene; as action against climate change cannot happen without persons and groups taking conscious initiatives to mitigate or adapt to the phenomenon. These stakeholders are critical to any action or inaction on climate change.

Against this backdrop, this book examines the climate action narrative in Nigeria with a focus on the key actors or stakeholders that enable and facilitate the country's compliance or non-compliance to her international commitments on climate change.

The book's focus on Nigeria as a developing nation is in contrast to the prevailing regime where climate action by developed and advanced countries receives more attention. As a party to UNFCCC, Nigeria agrees with the provisions of the convention which demands all parties to, "formulate, implement, publish and regularly update national and, where appropriate, regional programmes containing…measures to facilitate adequate adaptation to climate change" (UNFCCC 2014, Article 4.1b).

It is important that we acknowledge that the success of the UNFCCC is equally on developing countries. They too must provide information on their activities and level of compliance or non-compliance to the global regime on climate change. In agreement with Giddens "no amount of discussion at an international level will be of any consequence if… countries… do not make effective and radical responses to it" (Giddens, 2008, p. 3). Giddens further argues strongly in this line for a lead to be taken by governments of developing nations individually, to strategically develop policies and take actions that will encourage compliance to climate change agreements and reductions in emissions. This goes to demonstrate that, while the science of climate change is not in doubt, the governance of the subject constitutes a huge problem in the execution of climate action.

In the case of Nigeria, there is a dearth of standard texts discussing or analysing her climate action and its relation with the UNFCCC. This results to scarcity of data and uncertainty regarding the country's domestic action in line with her international commitments. There is also the allegation that climate change initiatives are indiscriminately executed by random actors, leading to loss of impact and difficulty to evaluate for improvement.

In the light of the above, this book is significant in several ways. From an empirical perspective, it exposes actions by stakeholders who influence the process. Given the current call for radical measures to reverse the impending climate emergency, the book projects a balanced picture of the state of climate action based on the assessment of select local experts. To a large extent this book will impact on the status of Nigeria's climate action on different scales. By exposing the factors driving climate action or inaction, this study is intended to engender more participation in the emerging green economy under the convention.

Conceptually, the book also brings academic focus on climate change governance in Nigeria as a political subject. This is to address the prevailing circumstance where the solution for the climate emergency in Nigeria is dominated by the scientific community. More importantly, this publication exposes potential areas for subsequent discussions and research on climate change in Nigeria. In terms of timeframe, the work generally focuses only on significant climate policy action since the inception of the UNFCCC up till 2016.

This book consisting of eleven chapters, is divided into three parts. Part one comprising chapters one to three, explains the concept of climate change and its governance in Nigeria. This section provides a background to the topic, an overview of the focus of the book and the motivation for embarking on this study. Here we discuss the subject of compliance in climate change as it relates to the UNFCCC.

Part two which starts from chapter four to chapter eight is on climate governance Stakeholders in Nigeria. This section presents and analyses quantitative and qualitative data on the key stakeholders driving climate change governance in Nigeria. It discusses data collated from field surveys and analyses Nigeria's performance regarding her climate change commitments. Using this integrated content analytic model, the book discusses and establishes the extent of Nigeria's compliance with her climate change commitments based on the activities of the critical stakeholders and independent evaluation by them.

Part three which consists of chapters nine, ten and eleven presents the prospects for improving climate governance in Nigeria. This section makes projections on the preferred direction for climate change governance actions by Nigeria vis-à-vis the global agenda on the issue. Hence the thesis here is centred on parts two and three especially, where domestic stakeholders and their climate action initiatives are discussed and analysed concurrently. It is from here that the book arrives at a conclusion and makes recommendations for policy action on climate change governance in the country.

CHAPTER TWO

CONCEPTUALISING CLIMATE GOVERNANCE

THE CONCEPT OF CLIMATE CHANGE

It is important to have conceptual clarity on the meaning of climate change as the term bears a plethora of interpretations. According to the US National Research Council (2010), climate change connotes significant change in weather pattern for at least ten years. Some literatures use the term global warming to describe 'climate change'. For example, NASA (2011) uses the term global warming to define climate change as average weather change or comparative weather variation over an extended term. So climate change entails both atmospheric cooling or warming over a significant period. Cooling or warming are variants of climate change. The current concern is that, human activities cause atmospheric warming and the developed countries are principally responsible for these through fossil based industrialisation. These activities release heat absorbing gases called greenhouse gases. The primary GHG are carbon dioxide, methane, nitrous oxide, perfluorocarbons, hydrofluorocarbon, sulphur hexafluoride (Hefron, 2015). Scientifically these gases carry the following formulae - carbon dioxide (CO_2), methane (CH_4), nitrous oxide (N_2O), perfluorocarbons (PFCs), hydrofluorocarbon (HFCs) and sulphur hexafluorides (SF_6). These are the most important gases that contribute to climate change. Nitrogentrifluoride (NF_3) and Hydrofluorinated ethers were later added after the Kyoto protocol. These gases hamper atmospheric cooling and invariably threaten the earth's life systems.

Table 2.1: GHG causing climate change

Greenhouse Gases	GWP
Carbondioxide	1
Methane (CH_4)	21
Nitrous Oxide (N_2O)	310
Hydro-fluorocarbons (HCFs)	150-11,700
Perfluorocarbons (PFCs)	6,500-9,200
Sulphur hexafluoride (SF_6)	23,000

Source: Mutevu (2010)

Figure 2.1: Percentage Contribution of GHG to Global Warming Over 100 Years Based On 1994 Emissions

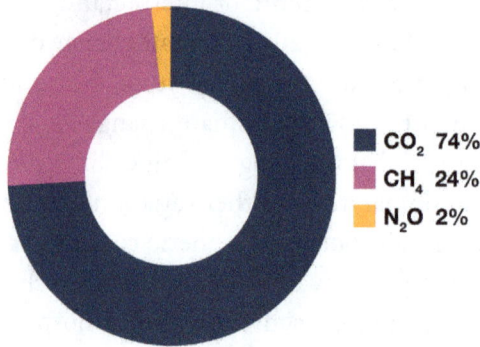

CO_2 74%
CH_4 24%
N_2O 2%

Source: FNC (2003)

On their part, developing countries negligibly contribute to climate change. Their main forcings emanate from obsolete industrialization, deforestation and uncontrolled urbanization. According to the Inter-governmental Panel on Climate Change, without GHG, the earth's surface would be about 15 degrees Celsius colder than the present average of 14 degrees Celsius. Since 2001, the IPCC acknowledges that if emission is stabilized, climate change will be reversed, but this will take a while. Climate impact will also vary for each country and even internally. This therefore calls for comprehensive solutions, taking cognizance of socio-economic vulnerabilities (Parry, Canzian, Palutiko, Vander Linken & Hansen, 2007).

Forecasts of these nature invite the attention of the global community for a way to reverse the trend. This is with a view to avert the catastrophic climatic consequences that would result from the build-up of these gases. Experts advise that mitigation action must be employed to reduce emission and concentration of these gases in the atmosphere. At the same time, the experts urge nations to brace for the impact of climate change by designing adaptive measures as survival strategy (IPCC, 1990). Thus, mitigation and adaptation are the scientific solutions to climate change and every country is invited to take concrete actions regarding these solutions as measures of compliance.

THE UNITED NATIONS FRAMEWORK CONVENTION ON CLIMATE CHANGE (UNFCCC)

Underscoring the universally catastrophic dimensions of climate change necessitated the need for a global context in addressing this scientific reality. Growing uproar over the human angle in global warming dragged the subject of climate change to the political front. Thus at the moment, research and discussions on climate change at the highest levels are predominantly shaped by the UN. Beginning with a UN conference on the human environment in Stockholm in 1972, the UN World Commission on Environment and Development was established in 1983. Under the leadership of the former Prime Minister of Norway, Dr. Gro Harlem Brundtland, the UN World Commission on Environment and Development in their report titled "our common heritage" published in 1987, called for a more concerted action from political leaders on the way to save the planet. The report for the first time brought to light, the relationship between climate action and sustainable development.

Following the Brundtland report, the World Meteorological Organisation and the United Nations Environmental Programme established the Intergovernmental Panel on Climate Change (IPCC) in 1988 to evaluate existing science on climate change related to man's actions and options for adaptation and mitigation. The submission by the IPCC in 1990 in its first assessment report was startling. It revealed that anthropogenic activities from emissions were increasing the concentration of GHG in the atmosphere and if not reversed, global mean temperatures would rise by 0.3 degrees celsius per decade. The results include melting ice caps and rising sea levels reaching 20 centimetres and 65 centimetres respectively between 2030 and 2100. The report suggested that reversing this trend would require dramatic actions, mainly cutting GHG emissions by 60%.

The conclusion of this report served as a foundation for negotiations under the United Nations General Assembly for a convention on climate change (Parry, Canzian, Palutiko, Van Der Linden, Pau, & Hansen, 2007). Shortly after, in 1992, the Earth Summit in Rio de Janeiro, Brazil, led to the establishment of the UNFCCC (effective in 1994) with 154 initial signatories- as state parties to the Convention. The UNFCCC is pursued with the objective of safely managing GHG in the atmosphere. Specifically, article 2 states, inter alia:

> The ultimate objective of this convention… is to achieve… stabilization of greenhouse gas concentrations in the atmosphere at a level that would prevent dangerous anthropogenic interference with the climate system. Such a level should be achieved within a timeframe sufficient to allow ecosystems to adapt naturally to climate change, to ensure that food production is not threatened and to enable economic development in a sustainable manner (UNFCCC, 1992).

Hence to achieve this objective, all countries have a general commitment to address climate change, adapt to its effects, and report their actions to implement the convention (UNFCCC Handbook, 2006). According to the convention, climate change and its adverse effect are constant threats to life forms on the planet. These are the result of human activities mainly by the developed countries, leading to unprecedented concentration of GHG in the atmosphere.

Acknowledging that climate change has taken a global dimension, the convention calls for cooperation to formulate effective response to the problem. Through regulatory provisions, the convention aims to maintain GHG in the atmosphere at levels that would not affect the environment adversely. Low lying states, small island states, low lying coastal and semi-arid areas, areas susceptible to flood, drought, desertification, land locked and transit states, states with high urban atmospheric pollution, developing countries, countries with mountainous ecosystems are recognized by the convention as negatively affected by climate change. In this regard, everyone is invited to be part of the process of combating climate change.

The UNFCCC enjoins "states to formulate, publish, implement and update national and regional regulations that mitigate climate change through anthropogenic emissions." When it comes to technologies and regulations to stop or reduce GHG, the UNFCCC promotes cooperation by states.

The Convention also recognizes the respective capacities to respond. For instance, developing countries are categorized as lacking the means wielded by their developed counterparts. Primarily, the convention expects developed countries to adopt national policies to mitigate climate change and to communicate these to the UNFCCC secretariat.

The need for legal regimes to institutionalize climate change measure are encouraged by the convention. States are also encouraged to embark on public awareness and make information on climate change accessible to all. These comprise climate change financing mechanisms, climate change research and transfer of technology, among others.

Three years after the convention was adopted in Rio de Janeiro, it became apparent that more needed to be done if the convention were to achieve its main objective of stabilizing GHG emissions at safe levels. Thus the orientation changed from non-quantifiable to the push for a legally binding commitment. The changing orientation considers that article 17 of the UNFCCC provides for the adoption of protocols to the convention. Consequently, in 1997 the Kyoto Protocol was adopted (UNFCCC Handbook, 2006) and the Paris Agreement in 2015 (Voight, 2016; Nandy, 2017).

The parties to the convention meet each year in the Conference of the Parties (COP) to assess progress in dealing with climate change (Ngoweh, 2016). Only parties to the convention participate in the protocols that strengthen and supplement the convention (Art. 17.4). The protocols reiterate the fundamental provisions of the convention with a few additions. The groupings and institutions of the convention are also applicable to the protocol with focus on developed countries. Quantified emissions are stipulated for developed countries and cost-effective flexible mechanisms for developing countries; joint implementation on projects for developed countries and a clean development mechanism for projects in developing countries (Bhullar, 2013). There is also the creation of the Adaptation Fund taking cognizance of increasing vulnerability (Bhullar, 2013).

Under the UNFCCC, developing countries in climate change discourse are referred to as non-annex I parties. According to the convention such countries only have general commitments to respond to climate change with a few voluntary obligations based on external support. "They are also required to provide a general description of steps taken or envisaged to implement the convention and estimate emissions of greenhouse gases" (UNFCCC, 2017). The developed countries or annex I parties include industrialised countries (members of the Organisation for Economic Cooperation and Development as of 1992 as well as Economies in Transition (UNFCCC, 2017). These countries accept prime responsibility for emissions (UNFCCC, 2017).

i. **Annex I** (Developed Industrialised and Economies in Transition) – Only cut down emissions.
ii. **Annex II** (Only Developed Industrialised) – Cut down emissions and support developing countries financially and technologically.

Non-annex I and II countries who are considered as developing, have no obligations under the Kyoto Protocol. Rather they are expected to benefit from the obligations of the developed countries and countries in transition.

Table 2.2: UN Classification of Developed Countries/Economies Annex I

Europe			Other countries	Major developed economies (G7)
European Union	New EU member States	Other Europe		
EU-15	Bulgaria	Iceland	Australia	Canada
Austria	Croatia	Norway	Canada	Japan
Belgium	Cyprus	Switzerland	Japan	France
Denmark	Czech Republic		New Zealand	Germany
Finland	Estonia		United States	Italy
France	Hungary			United Kingdom
Germany	Latvia			United States
Greece	Lithuania			
Ireland	Malta			
Italy	Poland			
Luxembourg	Romania			
Netherlands	Slovakia			
Portugal	Slovenia			
Spain				
Sweden				
United Kingdom				

Source: *WESP (2014)*

Table 2.3: Grouping of Non-Annex I Countries

Regions	Countries	Total	
		G-77	Non G-77
Africa	Algeria, Angola, Benin, Botswana, Burkina Faso, Burundi, Cameroon, Cape Verde, Central African Republic, Chad, Comoros, Congo (DR), Congo (Rep.), Cote d'Ivoire, Djibouti, Egypt, Equatorial Guinea, Eritrea, Ethiopia, Gabon, Gambia, Ghana, Guinea, Guinea-Bissau, Kenya, Lesotho, Liberia, Libya, Madagascar, Malawi, Mali, Mauritania, Mauritius, Morocco, Mozambique, Namibia, Niger, Nigeria, Rwanda, Sao Tome and Principe, Senegal, Seychelles, Sierra Leone, Somalia, South Africa, Sudan, Swaziland, Tanzania, Togo, Tunisia, Uganda, Western Sahara, * Zambia, Zimbabwe.	53	
Asia	Afghanistan, Armenia, * Azerbaijan, * Bahrain, Bangladesh, Bhutan, Brunei, Cambodia, China, Cyprus, Georgia, * India, Indonesia, Iran, Iraq, Israel, * Jordan, Kazakhstan, * Korea (DPR), Korea (Rep.), * Kuwait, Kyrgyzstan, * Lao (PDR), Lebanon, Malaysia, Maldives, Mongolia, Myanmar, Nepal, Oman, Pakistan, Palestine, lxxii Papua New Guinea, Philippines, Qatar, Saudi Arabia, Singapore, Sri Lanka, Syria, Tajikistan, * Thailand, Turkmenistan, United Arab Emirates, Uzbekistan, * Vietnam, Yemen.	36	9
Latin America and the Caribbeans	Antigua and Barbuda, Argentina, Bahamas, Barbados, Belize, Bolivia, Brazil, Chile, Costa Rica, Cuba, Colombia, Dominica, Dominican Republic, Ecuador, El Salvador, Grenada, Guatemala, Guyana, Haiti, Honduras, Jamaica, Mexico, * Nicaragua, Panama, Paraguay, Peru, St. Kitts and Nevis, St. Lucia, St. Vincent and the Grenadines, Suriname, Trinidad and Tobago, Uruguay, Venezuela.	32	1

Europe	Albania, * Andorra, * Bosnia Herzegovina, Holy See, * Macedonia (FYR), * Malta, Moldova, * San Marino, * Yugoslavia (Federal Rep.) *	2	7
Oceania	Cook Islands, * Fiji, Kiribati, * Marshall Islands, Micronesia (Federal States of), Nauru, * Niue, * Palau, * Samoa, Solomon Islands, Tonga, Tuvalu, * Vanuatu.	7	6
Total G-77	All the above countries minus the * ones, i.e. those mentioned below.	130	
Non-G-77	Albania, Andorra, Armenia, Azerbaijan, Cook Islands, Georgia, Holy See, Israel, Kazakhstan, Kiribati, Korea (Rep.), Kyrgyzstan, Macedonia (Former Yugoslav Republic of), Mexico, Nauru, Niue, Palau, Moldova, San Marino, Tajikistan, Tuvalu, Uzbekistan, Yugoslavia (Federal Rep.)		23

*South Sudan was not an independent state at the time of this publication

Source: Gupta (2008)

MITIGATION UNDER THE UNFCCC

The United Nations Environmental Programme (UNEP) defines mitigation as efforts to reduce or prevent emissions of greenhouse gases. "Mitigation can mean using new technologies and renewable energies, making older equipment more energy efficient or changing management practices or consumer behaviour." (climatechangedelhi, 2019). It encompasses simple farming methods and complex manufacturing systems. Through mitigation therefore, GHG causing global warming are controlled and reduced. Pielke (2009) states that mitigation can be achieved through two approaches viz i. reduced fossil fuel consumption ii. Reducing carbondioxide in the atmosphere by storing gas or its components elsewhere otherwise called carbon sequestration or carbon capture.

The first instance is achieved by reduction in fossil-based energy use or increase in renewable energy use. The developed countries have led the way in this regard. The UNFCCC admonishes the annex I countries to be the vanguards of mitigation action. Specifically, it states that,

> Each of these parties shall adopt national policies and take corresponding measures on the mitigation of climate change… these policies and measures will demonstrate that developed countries are taking the lead in modifying longer term trends in anthropogenic emission consistent with the objective of the convention (UNFCCC 1994, Art. 4a).

Since coming into effect of the UNFCCC, scientific milestones have been achieved in this area. Wind, solar and associated gases have been developed as sustainable energy sources. The European Union as a bloc leads in the application of renewable energy as a mitigation measure with Germany being the frontline country.

The second mitigation approach - carbon sequestration, calls for afforestation or tree planting as a natural bulwark to absorb carbon in the atmosphere through natural photosynthesis. Thus, the preservation and planting of trees keep emission from the atmosphere. Fast growing and young trees absorb huge amount of carbon from the atmosphere and store carbon atoms in new wood. Unfortunately, mitigation through carbon sequestration is under global threat (Mustapha, Yunusa & Mukhtar, 2015, p.65). Forests are being cleared in developed and developing countries at unprecedented levels. The worst experience is in the tropical regions where the earth crust is bleached by extreme anthropogenic activities. The outcome of these activities like fertilizer application, urban housing and bush fires lead to carbon emission.

In recognizing the indispensability of mitigation in reversing climate change, the UNFCCC at COP 12 in Bali agreed on a Nationally Appropriate Mitigation Action (NAMA) to be adopted by all countries as a reference point for mitigation. Though focused on developed countries, NAMA stipulates that based on equity, every country may engage in mitigation depending on its capability. This is in line with the principle of common but differentiated responsibilities. Going by the UNFCCC, developing countries' compliance to NAMA will depend on the fulfilment of their commitment by developed countries in terms of finance and technology transfer to the developing countries. This bears in mind that developing countries are already preoccupied with their socio-economic development which centres on poverty eradication. The guidelines for NAMA provide that developing countries have the leverage to decide and determine what mitigation approaches to adopt.

Mitigation therefore calls for behavioural change to conserve energy, use of energy sources that are renewable or have zero emission, energy efficient technology as well as carbon capture and storage (Michael & Stephen, 2008). Included in mitigation is the harnessing of green architecture for building and urban development. Here structural designs encompass efficient use of water, biofuels and renewable energy sources. Another mitigation initiative under the UNFCCC is the assigning of costs to carbon dioxide emission and placing value on the reduction of emission to provide economic incentives as a form of regulation. In other words, the establishment of carbon markets.

Under the UNFCCC, Mitigation measures constitute the greatest challenge to climate change as both developed and developing nations renege on the reduction of GHG emissions (Hoff and Gausset, 2015). Simply put, the question of the earth's vulnerability is more and more a function of non-mitigation. The initiatives of Certified Emission Reduction under the Clean Development Mechanism (CDM), Land Use Land Use Change and Forestry (LULUCF), Emission Reduction unit under Joint Implementation (JI) unit in the Kyoto Protocol, are all to promote mitigation This is in recognition of the reality that reduction of GHG through mitigation is at the heart of the survival of the planet in its current state.

ADAPTATION UNDER THE UNFCCC

Adaptation refers to actions taken to minimise the adverse effects of climate change (EC, 2016). It also refers to ecological, social and economic adjustments to the impact of climate change. Another definition for adaptation is the society's response to the impact of climate change (Muhammad, Shagari & Gatawa, 2012). Adaptation is the same as change in process, practice and structures in order to moderate or obstruct the potential or actual damage by climate change or even take advantage of the opportunities accompanying climate change (Ayoade, 2002). This comprises using scarce water more efficiently or adapting buildings in anticipation of extreme weather, developing drought tolerant crops, etc. To effectively manage the risk posed by climate change, adaptation is a necessary measure (Ford and Berrang-Ford, 2011). Having felt the impact of climate change, it is necessary for man to reconsider his lifestyle and action either as an individual, a society or a government. Through adaptation, the response is improved from vulnerability to resilience. Vulnerability here refers to unprotected exposure to climate change while resilience is the capacity to react positively or absorb the impact of climate change. To ensure adaptation, the UNFCCC compels members to develop a National Adaptation Plan of Action (NAPA).

Going by the above, it is self-evident that adaptation is needed to address the impact from global warming which is unavoidable because of increasing anthropogenic emissions. Thus, while there is uncertainty on future climate changes, it is imperative to invest in adaptation. The UNFCCC singles out adaptation as a priority area for all developing countries having identified these group of non-annex I countries as the most vulnerable. In 2001 all countries, especially developing countries were admonished to urgently take adaptation measures against climate change. Earlier on, the Adaptation Fund was instituted in 2000 and has been applied since 2008, to address concrete adaptation measures to the impact of climate change, most especially for developing countries.

According to Easterling (1999), there are two types of adaptation, these are autonomous adaptation and planned adaptation. In autonomous adaptation, changes in rainfall season force the farmer to naturally embrace different planting and sowing dates or a farmer may switch to crops that are suitable to the new climate. For example, a farmer sowing maize may switch to a faster maturing maize variety in a drought prone area or grow drought resistant crops like sorghum.

In planned adaptation, conscious policy options which are multi-sectoral in nature are aimed at improving the adaptive capacity of a population or society. This can be demonstrated in articulated building guidelines in small island states. Mendelsohn & Dinar (1999), assert that when adaptation is fully implemented, the impact of climate change is drastically reduced. They advise that such adaptation should be short or long term. Usually the short-term adaptations are autonomous while long-term adaptations are planned and multi-sectoral. Long term adaptation strategies involve major structural changes to overcome adversity in land use and techniques.

Because of developing countries reliance on natural resources and rain-fed agriculture, they are most challenged in terms of adaptive capacity. Adaptive capacity here is the ability to cope or recover from exposure to climate change otherwise called resilience. This capacity is dependent on wealth, political and social circumstances, infrastructure and even institutional support (Muhammad, Shagari & Gatawa, 2015). Given the above conditions, developing countries need to improve on their adaptive capacity which involves changes in lifestyle. This is a way resilience can be built to achieve sustained growth and development in the face of the disruptive nature of climate change. Adaptation is important because even when emissions are stabilized, it is scientifically established that climate change will persist for a while (Onafeso, Cornelius & Adegbayi, 2017).

COMPLIANCE IN CLIMATE CHANGE

Even though compliance with international agreements is principally considered a legal term, its origin and implications are highly political (Giddens, 2008). Given its political character, compliance suffers ambiguous interpretations which affects obedience or defiance. With this in mind, it is important to provide a conceptual clarification of compliance in international relations before arriving at its application to climate change.

Compliance is founded on a body of "laws applicable to the complex inter-related world community which begins with the individual and encompasses the so called family of nations or society of states (Koh, 1998, p.35). Based on this framework, states comply with international agreements through interaction, interpretation and internalization. In other words, compliance is purely based on judgment (Jacobson &

Weiss, 1995). Consequently, issues like characteristics of the activity, characteristics of the accord and even the international environment could affect compliance and frustrate the dictates of transnational law (Jacobson & Weiss, 1995).

From the above we can deduce that although compliance with agreements is the bedrock of international relations, it is always a complex process. For this reason, the quest to establish why states comply with international agreements including multilateral environmental agreements like that of climate change is always a pertinent subject. Guzman (2008, p.8) espouses that states in international relations comply with agreements for three reasons: reputation, reciprocity and retaliation. Under reputation, a state shows commitment to an agreement to propel its image on the international stage. Here states desirous of building relations with other states place a lot of value in being perceived as trustworthy. By reciprocity, parties to international agreement pursue mutual benefits. Through this, each state attains its objectives. Retaliation connotes the fear of violating an agreement to avoid a chain of reprisal moves by other state parties to the agreement. Guzman's postulation targets states as major parties to agreements. At the centre of Guzman's postulation is national interest by states. However, one can aver that non-state actors play significant roles in international agreement. On issues like climate change for instance, non-governmental organizations, private sector, indigenous peoples, etc, are actively involved. In fact these actors constitute the major stakeholders with positions on how the UNFCCC projects should be executed in respective countries (Onafeso, Cornelisu & Adegbayi 2017). As already observed above, such players also contribute to the complexity of compliance in international relations.

In terms of climate change the contention is between developing and developed countries and this is extended to compliance with agreements. But in effect, the environmental regimes include institutions or organisations that influence state behaviour and facilitate participation. For example, the IPCC is a working group of scientists that provides current research impact and guidance for global climate change mitigation and adaptation. Institutions like the World Bank and the Global Environmental Facility also participate in this environmental regime.

But regardless of the criticism, the UNFCCC is state-driven even though there are other actors. Both state and non state actors entertain the fear that complying fully with the UNFCCC entails taking drastic measures with unintended consequences. The resolution of this fear to the satisfaction of all actors is the silver veil for climate action. This will be a major step in the global compliance with the UNFCCC.

Building on this logic, Voigt (2017) submits that compliance under the UNFCCC should be distinguished from implementation. In this regard, she explains that while compliance is applicable when there is a binding international obligation, implementation refers to concrete measures by a state party taken to realize voluntary initiatives (Voigt, 2017, 162). On this note she lists the areas of obligation and voluntary commitment under the UNFCCC to comprise Mitigation, Adaptation, Finance, Technology Development and Transfer, Transparency of Action and Support, and Capacity building. Developing and developed countries are enjoined under the UNFCCC to commit to these areas in the fight against climate change. Voigt in her submission therefore advises that, if there must be headway in climate change action, countries must separate initiatives that arise as a result of obligation from those implementations that arise from voluntary initiatives. Simply put, Voigt's explanation clarifies the distinction we require in this study over what constitutes compliance. In essence, compliance only relates to international obligations on the subject of climate change. This is also validated by the United Nations Environmental Programme (UNEP) when it states that compliance is applied in international context while enforcement or implementation carries national context (UNEP, 2006, p.32). Both measures could be applied to address climate change. UNEP acknowledges that for any international agreement to be effective as a legal instrument, it has to be implemented by the parties. Jacobson and Weiss also give force to this in professing that international agreements can only be effective if implemented by the domestic legal system (Jacobson & Weiss, 1998).

The UNFCCC in recognizing the difficulty in guaranteeing compliance put in place two critical mechanism at the disposition of the state-parties viz i. Subsidiary Body For Science And Technology Advice (SBSTA) and ii. Subsidiary Body For Implementation (SBI). SBSTA is the link with the IPCC on the latest science on climate change including impacts and provides information and guidelines on technology acquisition and transfer. It also sets standards for preparing reports on greenhouse gas emissions. The SBI facilitates action on all agreements and treaties. In this role it relates directly with parties in taking concrete actions on climate change. These mechanisms under articles 9 and 10 of the convention are fundamental in states action on climate change. Annually, parties to the UNFCCC meet to negotiate and evaluate pending international commitments as well as proffer solutions on the way forward. These meetings are referred to as the annual Conference of Parties (COP). The COP brings together Heads of State and Governments as well as Climate Change experts to negotiate on the current challenges facing the global climate and initiatives to reverse the trend. Since the first COP 1 held in Berlin in 1995 at the inception of the UNFCCC, 24 Summits of the COP have been held around the globe by 2019, with each Summit announcing new international commitments towards combating climate change. Each COP has resulted in varying resolutions.

Table 2.4: Timeline of Meetings of UNFCCC Conference of Parties (COP) and Resolutions 1995-2016

City	Year	Conference of Party (COP) Series	Highlights
Berlin (Germany)	1995	COP 1	Parties agreed that mechanisms under the UNFCCC were inadequate and agreed to what would be called the Berlin Mandate, which allows parties to make specific commitments. Non-Annex 1 countries are exempted from additional obligations.
Geneva (Switzerland)	1996	COP 2	Attendees endorsed the results of the IPCC's second assessment report. The Geneva Ministerial Declaration, which in part called on parties to accelerate negotiations on a legally binding protocol, was noted, but not adopted.

Kyoto (Japan)	1997	COP 3	The Kyoto Protocol was adopted by consensus with more than 150 signatories. The Protocol included legally binding emissions targets for developed country Parties for the six major GHGs, which are carbon dioxide, methane, nitrous oxide, hydrofluorocarbons, perfluorocarbons, and sulfur hexafluoride. The Protocol offered additional means of meeting targets by way of three market-based mechanisms: emissions trading, the Clean Development Mechanism (CDM), and Joint Implementation (JI).
Buenos Aires (Argentina)	1998	COP 4	Parties adopted the Buenos Aires Plan of Action, allowing a two year period to develop mechanisms for implementing the Kyoto Protocol. The COP also decided to review the financial mechanism of the Convention every four years.
Bonn (Germany)	1999	COP 5	Parties continued negotiation efforts with a focus on "the adoption of the guidelines for the preparation of national communications by [developed] countries, capacity building, transfer of technology and flexible mechanisms.
Hague (Netherland)	2000	COP 6	Negotiations faltered, and parties agreed to meet again in Bonn.
Marrakech (Morocco)	2001	COP 7	The detailed rules for the implementation of the Kyoto Protocol were adopted and called the Marrakesh Accords. The Special Climate Change Fund (SCCF) was established to "finance projects relating to: adaptation; technology transfer and capacity building; energy transport, industry, agriculture, forestry and waste management; and economic diversification." The Least Developed Countries Fund was also "established to support a work programme to assist Least Developed Country Parties (LDCs) carry out, inter alia [among other things], the preparation and implementation of national adaptation programmes of action (NAPAs).
New Delhi (India)	2002	COP 8	Parties adopted the Delhi Ministerial Declaration that, among other things, called for developed countries to transfer technology to developing countries.

Milan (Italy)	2003	COP 9	New emisssions reporting guidelines based on IPCC recommendations were adopted. The Special Climate Change Fund (SCCF) and the Least Developed Countries Fund (LDCF) were further developed.
Buenos Aires (Argentina)	2004	COP 10	Parties began discussing adaptation options. The parties "addressed and adopted numerous decisions and conclusions on issues relating to development and transfer of technologies; land use, land use change and forestry; the UNFCCC's financial mechanism; [developed countries'] national communications; capacity building; adaptation and response measures; and UNFCCC Article 6 (education, training and public awareness) examining the issues of adaptation and mitigation, the needs of least developed countries (LDCs), and future strategies to address climate change."
Montreal (Canada)	2005	COP 11	The parties addressed issues such as "capacity building, development and transfer of technologies, the adverse effects of climate change on developing and least developed countries, and several financial and budget-related issues, including guidelines to the Global Environment Facility (GEF)."
Nairobi (Kenya)	2006	COP 12	Financial mechanisms were reviewed, and further decisions were made about the Special Climate Change Fund.
Bali (Indonesia)	2007	COP 13	Parties agreed to a Bali Action Plan to negotiate GHG mitigation actions after the Kyoto Protocol expires in 2012. The Bali Action Plan did not require binding GHG targets for developing countries.
Poznan (Poland)	2008	COP 14	Countries began negotiations on the financing mechanism to help poor countries adapt to the effects of climate change. Negotiations continued about what would succeed the Kyoto Protocol.

Copenhagen (Denmark)	2009	COP 15	Leaders from the United States, Brazil, China, Indonesia, India and South Africa agreed to what would be called the Copenhagen Accord which recognized the need to limit the global temperature rise to 2°C based on the science of climate change. While no legally binding commitments were required by the deal, countries were asked to pledge voluntary GHG reduction targets. $100 billion was pledged in climate aid to developing countries.
Cancun (Mexico)	2010	COP 16	Parties officially adopted major tenets of the Copenhagen Accord including limiting global warming to 2°C, protecting vulnerable forests, and establishing a framework for a Green Climate Fund meant to deliver funds to developing countries for mitigation and adaptation actions.
Durban	2011	COP 17	Parties agreed to the Durban Platform for Enhanced Action which is framework to establish a new international emissions reduction protocol. Under the Durban Platform, the details of the new protocol are to be finalized by 2015 and it will come into force in 2020.
Doha (Qatar)	2012	COP 18	Parties agreed to extend the expiring Kyoto Protocol, creating a second commitment phase that would begin on January 1, 2013 and end December 31, 2020. This is considered as a bridge to the Durban Platform for Enhanced Action, agreed upon in 2011, and set to come into force in 2020. Parties failed to set a pathway to provide $100 billion per year by 2020 for developing countries to finance climate change adaptation, as agreed upon at COP 15 in Copenhagen. The concept of "loss and damage" was introduced as developed countries pledged to help developing countries and small island nations pay for the losses and damages from climate change that they are already experiencing.

Warsaw (Poland)	2013	COP 19	Differences of opinion on responsibility of GHG emissions between developing and developed countries led to a flexible ruling on the wording and a plan to discuss further at the COP 20 in Peru. A non-binding agreement was reached among countries to set up a system tackling the "loss and damage" issue, although details of how to set up the mechanism were not discussed. Concerning climate finance, the United Nations' Reducing Emissions from Deforestation and Forest Degradation (REDD+) Program, aimed at preserving the world's forests, was formally adopted.
Lima (Poland)	2014	COP 20	Differences of opinion on responsibility of GHG emissions between developing and developed countries led to a flexible ruling on the wording and a plan to discuss further at the COP 20 in Peru. A non-binding agreement was reached among countries to set up a system tackling the "loss and damage" issue, although details of how to set up the mechanism were not discussed. Concerning climate finance, the United Nations' Reducing Emissions from Deforestation and Forest Degradation (REDD+) Program, aimed at preserving the world's forests, was formally adopted.
Paris (France)	2015	COP 21	The UNFCCC reached a landmark agreement to combat climate change and to accelerate and intensify the actions and investments needed for a sustainable low carbon future. The Paris Agreement builds upon the Convention and – for the first time – brings all nations into a common cause to undertake take ambitious efforts to combat climate change and adapt to its effects, with enhanced support to assist developing countries to do so. As such, it charts a new course in the global climate effort.
Marrakech	2016	COP 22	The Marrakech Action Proclamation was made by heads of state, governments and delegations at COP22. The Proclamation acknowledges that 2016 has seen extraordinary momentum on climate change in many fora and calls for the highest political commitment to combatting climate change. It calls for urgently raising ambition. Developed countries reaffirmed their commitment to a mobilisation of USD100bn for climate finance.

Source: Adapted from UNFCCC (2016)

CHAPTER THREE

NIGERIA AND THE UNFCCC AGREEMENTS

OVERVIEW OF NIGERIA'S ENVIRONMENTAL POLICIES

Climate change is one issue that threatens to increase the vulnerability of nations all over the world. The establishment of UNEP in the late 1980s has seen environmental issues gradually taking centre stage in some countries' development plans. Chapter 2 Article 28 of the 1999 Constitution of the Federal Republic of Nigeria declares that "the state shall protect and improve the environment and safeguard the water, air and land, forest and wildlife of Nigeria" (FGN Constitution, 1999). But even before the proclamation of the 1999 Constitution and the emergence of climate change as a subject of global concern, the issue of gas flaring and oil spillage were already precursors to eventual climate change conundrum.

Since the late 1960s there had been various governmental initiatives to deal with environmental problems. A military government enacted a petroleum decree in 1969 which prescribed a preliminary market study before exploitation of oil and gas. A decree imposed by the Obasanjo military government in the late 70s, enjoined that all gas flaring activities were to mandatorily end by 1984. No oil company complied (Koblowsky & Speranza, 2010). In 1988, the Federal Environmental Protection Agency (FEPA) was created with a mandate to articulate standards in all environmental matters. Later, the National Environmental Policy of 1989 identified Nigeria's key environmental needs as air and water pollution, urban decay, municipal waste, coastal surges, land degradation, deforestation, desertificaction, flood as well as coastal and marine environmental erosion (Ati, Agubamah & Abaje, 2018, p.113). Subsequently, the Environmental Impact Assessment decree was enacted in 1992, coinciding with the period of the Rio Summit that resulted in the establishment of the UNFCCC in 1992.

FEPA and its accompanying environmental policy remain the turning point in Nigeria's environmental policy (Koblowsky & Speranza, 2010). These laid the foundation for subsequent environment related directives and institutional innovations leading to the country's accession to the UNFCCC in 1992 and ratification in 1994. The UNFCCC contains commitments for developed and developing countries. Nigeria's ratification of the document in 1994 entails that the country is obligated to comply through implementation. In the UNFCCC document, article 3, article 4, article 5, article 6 and article 12 contain clauses that target developing countries (UNFCCC, 1992). Herein lies Nigeria's commitments under the convention. In the document, these commitments are divided into specific and general obligations (UNFCCC, 1992). These articles pertain to different concerns of the framework.

UNFCCC ARTICLE 3 VIS-À-VIS NIGERIA'S DOMESTIC SCENARIO

This article deals with the guiding principles of the agreement and only bears general commitments for all parties. It sets the ground rules for the convention as it calls on both developed and developing countries to take precautionary measures to prevent or minimize the adverse effects of climate change (Art.3.3). The article also invites developed countries to render assistance to developing countries bearing in mind the disproportionate climate impact on the latter. It therefore calls for cooperation among states to uphold sustainable climate friendly development (Art. 3.5).

In proffering actionable measures to address article three, the 2012 IPCC special report stipulates that state-parties through diverse agencies should raise awareness on climate variability and change in the location and design of waste water infrastructure; as well as environmental monitoring for flood early warning (IPCC 2012 in Field et al). Noting the above concern in article 3, the National Policy on Drought and Desertification emphasises the need to equip relevant agencies, institutions and citizens adequately to collect, analyze and use climate data effectively to ameliorate and combat drought and desertification (Oladipo, 2010).

While acknowledging the merits of the drought policy, Oladipo still laments that Nigeria has no clear policy directed at coastal zone management. He accuses the country of only participating in some respects in the implementation of the UNDP/UNEP/UNIDO/GEF project on combatting coastal area degradation and living resources depletion in the Guinea Current Large Marine Ecosystem (GCLME). This project has the potential to address priority trans-boundary problems in the area of anticipatory adaptation response to climate-induced changes to the coastal environment in Nigeria.

Oladipo (2010) also states that Nigeria's National Biodiversity Strategy and Action Plan aims to integrate biodiversity into national planning, policy and decision-making processes. Through this, the quality of the country's biological ecosystem will be improved by addressing biodiversity conservation, sustainable use of biological resources, equitable sharing of benefits, conservation of agro-biodiversity, biosafety and biodiversity-industry interface. These are essential roles in moderating the global carbon cycle and, therefore, climate.

It is pertinent to clarify that parts of Oladipo's critique have their limitations. For example, his critique that the country lacks policy on flood management in response to climate change is inaccurate. There is an existing policy on flood control in Nigeria. In fact, Adegbulugbe (2003) in acknowledging the existence of the policy, notes that the goal of the National Erosion and Flood Control Policy is to ensure coordinated and systematic measures in the management and control of climate-related hazards and risks of erosion and floods. As evident, all these would have significant implications for climate change adaptation measures that would need to be adopted to increase people resilience. Nevertheless, a major substance that must be taken from Oladipo's argument is that Nigeria's policy development measured against article 3 in addressing climate change remains a major challenge.

UNFCCC ARTICLE 4 VIS-À-VIS NIGERIA'S DOMESTIC SCENARIO

This article is the heart of the convention. It addresses commitments by both developed and developing countries. The article separates general and specific commitments for developed and developing countries as well. As a developing country, Nigeria's commitments are subsumed under Art. 4.1a-d. For example, Art. 4.1 takes cognizance of common but differentiated responsibilities of parties which affect their capacity to comply with the agreements. Based on this article, all states are advised to periodically develop and publish inventories of emissions and removals by sinks, development and cooperation in clean technology and conservation initiatives.

The same article also enjoins developed countries "to meet the agreed full costs incurred by developing countries in complying with their commitments under Art. 12 paragraph 1" (Art. 4.3). Here the finance for technology transfer and implementation of climate change measures by developing countries are stated as the responsibilities of developed countries. This also includes cost of adaptation. Art. 4.5 calls for "developed countries' to support "the enhancement of indigenous capacity and technologies of developing country parties".

From the various analyses of Adegbulugbe (2003), the enabling environment exists for the application of article 4 in Nigeria, especially in energy. This should be expected, since Nigeria has been a signatory of the convention from its inception over 25 years ago. A few initiatives with immense potentials in the energy sector have been identified. In the industrial sector, there is the opportunity to transition from fuel-oil to natural gas in the production of cement. There is also potential for the use of energy efficient motors as production machines. In households, the use of energy efficient fluorescent bulbs and fully efficient kerosene stoves are seen as viable initiatives that could be supported domestically by developed countries (Ibitoye & Akinbami, 1999). This is bearing in mind the provisions of article 4.7 that:

the extent to which developing country parties will effectively implement their commitments under the convention will depend on the effective implementation by developed country parties of their commitments related to financial resources and transfer of technology and will take fully into account that economic and social development and poverty eradication are the first and overriding priorities of the developed country parties (Art. 4.7)

Under specific commitments for developing countries like Nigeria, Art.4.1 (e-f) highlights the need for cooperation in adaptation measures as it affects agriculture and water resources, as well as protection of drought and flood prone areas. This article specifically invites countries to take climate change into account in policies and actions related to social, economic and environmental issues. The issue of impact assessment of projects to mitigate or adapt to climate change is categorically highlighted under this clause (4.1f).

To an extent Nigeria has made efforts to establish climate friendly policies under this article. Towards meeting the challenges of addressing the key environmental problems and challenges of land degradation, air and water pollution, urban decay and municipal waste, as well as drought, coastal surges, floods and erosion, the Nigerian government articulated a National Environmental Policy in 1989. The policy was revised in 1999. The country also enacted specific policies and action plans for the implementation of the National Environment Policy. There are policies on drought and desertification, biodiversity, agriculture, water and specific environmental threats. Adegbulugbe (2003) further provides clarification on two of these. In Nigeria's agricultural policy, the framework captures many issues that may be impacted by climate change. They include crops, livestock, fisheries and agro-forestry production, pest control, water resources and irrigation. National Water Policy, the framework seeks to improve on the nation's water resources management, including the management of hydrological risks and vulnerabilities. There is also emphasis on the assessment of water resources to improve real time forecasting of hydrological phenomena.

This major adaptation measure is required to reduce societal vulnerability to the impacts of climate change.

Also under specific obligations, article 4 calls on developed countries to assist with funding, insurance and technology transfer to the following categories of developing countries viz: small island states, low lying coastal areas, semi-arid areas, forested areas and areas liable to forest decay, areas prone to natural disasters, areas liable to drought and desertification, areas with high urban atmospheric pollution, areas with fragile ecosystem, landlocked and transit countries, as well as those whose economies are highly dependent on income generated from production, processing and or consumption of fossil fuels and associated energy intensive products. A perusal of these countries indicates a few corollaries with Nigeria's situation. Art. 4.10 also requests similar assistance for countries whose economies are highly dependent on income generated from production of fossil fuels which again applies to Nigeria. The consensus among scholars on this aspect of article 4 is that assistance from developed countries to Nigeria have never been sufficient to address her climate change challenges (Ayoade, 2004; Batta, Ashong & Bashir, 2013; Tarfa, 2017). In specific terms, the climate action interventions of developed countries in Nigeria have been mostly driven by NGOs from developed countries. Unfortunately, these non-profit organisations are financially constrained in funding clean energy initiatives or community wide adaptation measures that would result in significant transformation. The areas of concern here relate to the issues of hardware like technology transfer, knowledge capacity and infrastructure (Hussein & Karaye, 2015).

UNFCCC ARTICLE 5 VIS-À-VIS NIGERIA'S DOMESTIC SCENARIO

Article 5 centres on research and systematic observation. The article also contains general and specific obligation for Nigeria as a developing country. As a general commitment all parties are enjoined to generate data through systematic observation. There is also the call to support international and national research capacities especially in developing countries. Under specific obligations, the article enjoins developing countries to cooperate in improving their capacities relative to their needs. On Nigeria's action on article 5, it is instructive to inform that through her communications to the UNFCCC in the First National Communication (2003), Second National Communication (2014) and Nationally Determined Contribution (2016), Nigeria has taken steps to generate data on the status of climate change and related activities in the country. The data were prepared with inputs from the private sector and the civil society (Isaac, 2017). The UNDP, using NGOs in partnership with the Federal Ministry of Environment has over the years invested in the collection and validation of GHG data for the exercise. The same approach is being adopted in preparation for the third national communication (TNC). The TNC will focus on options for GHG reduction in all sectors (Isaac, 2017).

According to Anwadike (2017) the Nigerian Government has taken the issues of environmental degradation seriously by putting various national efforts in place. These are reflected at all levels of governance to promote environmental sustainability in the context of national sustainable development. He says Government recognizes that effective environmental governance is critical for sustainable development. Furthermore, specific agencies have been created to provide more focused attention to some specific environmental problems. They include the National Oil Spill Detection and Response Agency (NOSDRA) and National Environmental Standards and Regulations Enforcement Agency (NESREA), which were created in 2006 and 2007 respectively. NOSDRA has the mandate to implement the national oil spill contingency plan. NESREA has responsibility to enforce all environmental laws, guidelines, policies, standards and regulations in Nigeria, as well as enforce compliance with the provisions of all international agreements, protocols and conventions, treaties on the environment to which Nigeria is a signatory. From 2007 to 2012, NESREA developed 24 Environmental Regulations which have been gazetted and are in various stages of operationalization. These Regulations have key provisions for environmental control, clean-up and remediation. Other institutions include the Forestry Research Institute of Nigeria (FRIN), National Parks and Environmental Health Officers Registration Council of Nigeria (EHORECON). FRIN is mandated to conduct research into all aspects of Forestry, Wildlife Management,

Agro-Forestry and Forest Products Utilization, as well as train technical and sub-technical personnel for the forestry and agro-allied services in the country through its colleges.

Using the First National Communication (FNC) as a reference point, analysis by Adegbulugbe (2003) shows that afforestation could be the most effective mitigation measure for Nigeria in the land use change and forestry as mitigation action. Under the guidance of the African Union Commission, Nigeria is implementing the project on the "Great Green Wall Initiative" by which a "green wall" of trees (40 million trees annually in the next 10 years) will be planted across the dry-land area of Nigeria to not only push back deforestation and secure agriculture and livelihoods across the Sudano-Sahelian zone of the country, but also to enhance the carbon sequestration of biological-diversity resources in the region for climate change mitigation.

But more climate action initiatives in Nigeria are still desired compared to other African countries. According to Oladipo (2010) preliminary comparison of the adaptation capacities between Nigeria and Ghana, two West African countries, indicates that a programmatic approach is imperative to drive national adaptation process. This is necessary for mainstreaming climate action into national development and creating evidence-based actions that can reduce the vulnerability and enhance the resilience of the people to the impacts of climate change. Ghana has obviously performed better than Nigeria in terms of specifically having a National Climate Change Adaptation Strategy and detailed vulnerability assessment reports on land management, agriculture (cocoa and root tubers), water (fisheries), health and gender (Oladipo 2010). These studies are being used to determine necessary policy changes needed in agriculture, water, forestry and housing for effective adaptation to climate change. In a similar manner, the reports of the Technology Needs Assessment and Financial Needs provide Ghana evidence-based information for good policy decision-making. Many of these are still missing in Nigeria, although the country's climate action focal point keeps on indicating that they are at different levels of development. Oladipo therefore concludes that it will do Nigeria a lot of good if she takes more actionable initiatives compared to official statements just like we see in Ghana and sister African countries.

When it comes to flood control for instance, there are alternative approaches like the Limpopo basin of Mozambique, which combines several measures for flood management. Here, close to the farming lowlands, they have elevated settlements which protect the populace in extreme weather (Spaliviero, Dapper & Malo, 2011). In Kenya and Malawi, farmers erect metal silos as protection from physical and biological damages (SNC, 2014). This aspect of intervention by way of such storage facilities is yet to be fully explored in Nigeria to conquer the effect of rodents, intense rains and temperature in Agricultural communities.

UNFCCC ARTICLE 6 VIS-À-VIS NIGERIA'S DOMESTIC SCENARIO

Under article 6, Nigeria only has general commitments as a developing country. The clauses here address relative capacity building. The issue of open access to information on climate change and its effect, creation of public awareness programs on climate change, public participation in climate change matters as well as manpower development on climate matters are itemized here as general commitments to all parties with a plea for international cooperation where possible. In all these, developing countries are identified for special attention. With assistance from NGOs much has been achieved in this area (Koblosky, 2015). Climate change awareness is gradually gaining currency in the public space including schools and media organisations (Batta, Ashong & Bashir, 2013). However, the complaint has been that the focus on publicity is mitigation which is capital intensive and which should not be the focus for developing countries (Ukonu, Akpan & Anorue, 2012). The scholarly call in Nigeria is for vigourous publicity on adaptive measures to support life and livelihood as efforts and resources are mobilized for subsequent mitigation (Ayoade, 2004).

UNFCCC ARTICLE 12 VIS-À-VIS NIGERIA'S DOMESTIC SCENARIO

Article 12 pertains to communication of information related to implementation. The article generally invites every party to the convention to communicate national inventory of anthropogenic emissions by sources and removal by sinks based on its capacity.

What can be drawn from the above is that, developing countries may on a voluntary basis, propose projects, seek to finance technology, techniques or practices to implement the projects. Developed countries are enjoined to submit initial communication within six months of entry into force of the convention, while developing countries's communication is based on availability of financial resources. For Nigeria as a developing country, this provision is similar to the provisions in article 5 of the convention of which Nigeria's efforts are reflected in the FNC, SNC and NDC. However, her capacity to collate accurate data is highly constrained. Tarfa (2017) attributes this to poor technology and infrastructure. Relying on common but differentiated responsibility under the UNFCCC, Nigeria's limitations in this respect can be excused.

In general, we can see that the effectiveness of environmental policies in facilitating adaptation and mitigation measures in Nigeria are yet to be fully realized. A keen observer would notice that most of the policies remain broad and are unable to provide the required response to climate change concerns. It is rather unfortunate that while climate change is mentioned in some government policy documents, there is yet to be a definite policy action on climate change adaptation and mitigation. The country is still in a conundrum where the policy framework for aligning human development and climate change management remains largely undeveloped. To break from this lukewarm approach, there is a need to adapt existing national policies, strategies and plans to address climate change response.

Going through Nigeria's obligations under the UNFCCC, it is evident that the country's commitments are only voluntary and based on local benchmarks set by her. In other words, Nigeria's commitment is non-binding. It is adaptation that is emphasised for developing countries that have the means to do so. Thus, the UNFCCC makes it obligatory for Nigeria to develop strategies for adaptation and implementation with the support of developed countries. Nigeria as a developing country is enjoined by the UNFCCC to act on adaptation and communicate her climate change intensions to the UNFCCC secretariat. Consequently, under the UNFCCC, Nigeria can only be held responsible on her national communications and nationally determined contribution to climate change. Unfortunately, Nigeria has not been able to fulfil many of her voluntary commitments on adaptation as contained in these documents presented to the UNFCCC.

CHAPTER FOUR

DOMESTIC STAKEHOLDERS AS SOCIAL FORCES DRIVING CLIMATE GOVERNANCE

STAKEHOLDERS AS SOCIAL FORCES

Stakeholders refer to entities that are affected or concerned about a problem. So who are the stakeholders driving climate action? This study views climate actors under the auspices of social forces driving climate action. To interrogate why these stakeholders are considered as social forces therefore calls for an exhaustive discussion of the nexus between the concepts.

According to Fairchild (in Rummel, 1976) social force is any agent of social action. In short, there is social force when momentum is built among members of society to actually stimulate some type of action or change. In plural relationships, these forces form coalitions or groups. Classical American sociologist, A.W. Small distinguishes between two connotations of social forces. For the social worker and social reformer he says, the term refers to persons, institutions and groups who must be "taken into account either as obstacles to circumvent or resources to be mobilized in connection with a particular and concrete problem" (Park & Burgess, 2007). This is different from the definition ascribed by historians, who view social forces as the main lines of change which are distinct in the history of a particular state or area in a given period of interest (Park & Burgess, 2007). Social forces being currents of change must continue in the same direction for a significant period, different from what was obtainable before, until they are disrupted by a new factor that changes the direction of things.

For Small, the historian's conception are not far-fetched. First, he notes that the historian's perspective is a far cry from that of the social worker. As an explanatory paradigm, the historian does not see any difference between what a social worker considers as social force and the way the politician will view the same subject (Short in Zirra, 2019). While the social worker may consider the social force as an enabler of progress, the politician will view the same as a problem that threatens the establishment. Rather than pitch his ideological leaning with either of the groups, Small advocates that both definitions are useful in the study of any social phenomenon.

Thus, by social forces, we can mean;

> relatively few class names or categories, causal factors, tendencies, motives or pressures which are more or less universally at work in the social process and in all self-contained group processes or in the measure that they are self-contained. These general categories of causal forces are understood to be such that we may reasonably hope to be able to interpret a given concrete social situation (House, 1925, p.4)

Through the work of House, we see that central to the concept of social forces are social phenomena and social movement (in Zirra, 2019). By social phenomena he means a subject of concern affecting many factors which we need to know as a group or as individuals, as the phenomenon can materialize in special cases under consideration. Social movement here refers to the natural force of humanity which cannot be exhausted. This movement has always accounted for human advancement. As a corollary, we can add here that the chances of a social force being successful depends on its ability to judge issues and adjust as realities change, bearing in mind that governments generally desire to remain a step ahead of social forces (Scott, 2016 p. 11).

Essentially, House' concept of social forces demonstrate that every social incident is determined by forces that are not just internal. Bearing in mind that every social situation is the outcome of everything that exists, changing the situation requires one to adjust the existing configuration of forces and replace them with new factors. The role of these social forces is therefore central in comprehending any social situation.

Another scholar, Short, provides a holistic understanding of social forces as he clarifies that social forces do not operate in isolation. Hence there are usually external influences on their activities or emergence. He asserts that social forces operate as a network, because they "make claims that directly or indirectly impinge other groups...they have complex ...relationships with other groups that become allies and opponents...they also mobilize within institutional settings that structure conflict and possible outcomes" (Zirra, 2019 p.65). Scott (2016) notes elsewhere that, social forces also require resources to survive and grow, which in most cases come from external sources. This means that it will be unwise to look at social forces only from their internal dynamics within a state. In the analysis of the activities or the operations of such groups, it would not be out of place to view their internal dynamics vis-à-vis the broader perspective. Domestic and subjective activities of social forces are better appreciated within a broader complexity. We should not forget that having emerged from a broader context and attained some level of autonomy domestically or within a context, a social force acts, reacts and is affected by the broader external forces. We see this situation demonstrated daily in the cases of gay and lesbian movements around the world. Other instances of media freedom and the campaign for women and girls or any marginalized group, manifest the relationship between domestic social forces and their network in a broader context.

In Short's academic view, public opinion plays a major role in this web of relationship between social forces and their networks which have traces in political parties, media and even several levels of the state. It is this public opinion that determines the impact on the broader society (in Zirra, 2019). At this point, the media as the main public opinion is considered a formidable social force. It was the media's interest in the engagements of American civil rights activists in the 60s that significantly impacted on the broader society while the group of media that were not interested in this phenomenon lost its influence on society as a critical force. In the same vein, the world has witnessed domestic forces aligning with foreign counterparts to mobilize public opinion. In the US for instance, the civil rights struggle was predominantly a domestic affair, until the involvement of the communist party in the case of the Scottsboro Bays, resulting in mass protest around the world such as demonstrators engaging the police in Germany. This global impact galvanized the National Association for the Advancement of Coloured People (NAACP) to mobilize the black community around a cause in a way that was unprecedented in the United States (Scott in Zirra, 2019). Russia's signing of the Kyoto Protocol on Climate Change that came into force in 2005 was also the outcome of monumental pressure from opposition parties backed by external action from international Non-Governmental Organization. Such solidarity amongst external and internal forces influence public opinion and affect the direction of policy. The stand of Short here is that, social forces are bolstered by other groups both local and international.

Given the prevailing evidence illustrated above, social forces in this research refer to major actors in climate change policy or action in Nigeria including their strength and competences. This is drawing from the fact that Climate Change is a cross cutting issue that requires much integration across several government departments and stakeholders, as well as integration across sectors of industry, business and community (Koblowsky & Speranza, 2010).

SOCIAL FORCES IN NIGERIA

As Nigeria progressively participates in the global coalition against global warming, certain social factors have emerged as significant stakeholders in determining Nigeria's response to her climate change commitments. This brings afore the established assumptions in the social sciences that particular social structures give rise to social forces whose actions, politics, and ideologies shape institutional development. As we have seen earlier, these social forces refer to social groups that may have either formal or informal organizational features and that have shared interests. They may be social classes in the classic understanding of the term, defined by their relationship to the means of production (peasants, workers, for example), fractions of social classes, groups claiming religious or ethnic identities, or social movements (Teichman, 2012, 45).

It follows therefore that state bureaucracy or factions within it may come to constitute a social force. What this means is that, social force comprises all such groups that collectively or individually can have a powerful impact on social outcomes. The development of centralized, and efficacious state institution depends on the strength or weakness and configuration of these social forces. Such forces, otherwise called social groups, abide in every society. It is only natural that Nigeria's aspiration as an oil producing country in the third world participating in climate change agreements, must necessarily create social forces that frustrate or encourage her ability to meet set target.

Social forces may exert power due to their control of substantial resources, whether land or other capital assets—such is the case for big business interests and big landowners. However, labour groups, peasantries, and social movements, although lacking the same level of resources, may also act in an organized and combative manner (Teichman, 2012). Hence, a social force's effective strength determines the way in which it operates and the condition of other social forces. Thus, the influence of a social force with the most material resources may be hamstrung by the militancy of opposing social forces. In this vein, a social force that is numerically large but politically quiescent, may nevertheless affect outcome because a sympathetic political leadership recruits its support. In the end, Social forces and the state are key actors in the creation and perpetuation of inequality as well as the ability of a nation to implement any policy or agreement.

The emergence of social forces in Nigeria's polity is traceable to the country's colonial past when resources were administered along ethnic lines (Kalejaiye & Aliyu, 2013). The pre-independence period consolidated this colonial creation as political unions and associations were formulated based on affinity to kinship. The ability of these associations to exert influence on state affairs in the urban areas further resulted in the proliferation of communal associations. This attracted a large proportion of urban dwellers, triggering intra-class and inter-individual socioeconomic competition, especially among the various town unions. Nnoli (1978) succinctly explains the circumstance above in his claim that the scarcity of resources coupled with the failure of the state to provide employment and other services to the citizenry boosted the importance of these unions as legitimate social forces. As the bond between the individual and the union became stronger, loyalty was transferred from the state to the union which gave meaning to social existence. Switching loyalty also comes with benefits and this adds to the distance between the individual and the government (Nnoli, 1978). Sometimes, both the individual and the unions joined forces to fight the state for resources. With the passage of time, interest groups emerged as forces in their own right, advocating for different agenda (Abimbola, 2002). Non-Governmental Organisations, cultural associations and professional groups in Nigeria later emerged as social forces to influence policy and governance.

Progressively, social forces in the country penetrated the state to different degrees and through different mechanisms. For instance, they may gain access to the state by means of a client relationship with a bureaucrat or politician, or they may secure direct representation within the state through membership in a government body. Differing degrees and modes of incorporation would have important implications for policy and distributional outcomes. Given the intense relationship/friction between social forces and states, public policy and action in most cases is the outcome of bargain between the state and social forces. States may succeed in subjugating social forces or incorporating them, or powerful social forces may thoroughly penetrate and manipulate the state (Migdal, Kohli & Shue, 1994, p.25). In Nigeria, social forces emerge as interest groups or pressure groups (Abimbola, 2002). The interest of such groups is to consciously influence public policy or the authoritative allocation of values, and to move in a particular, general or specific direction (Abimbola, 2002, p.1). According to Perry (1976, p. 584-585), "social forces are many and varied and can be formally and informally organized. The more formally organized forces tend to be the more durable, whereas those informally organised usually dissolve after the crisis that originated them is resolved". It is important therefore to underscore that the lifespan and dedication to their causes are instrumental to making such a group functional. Based on their goals, they articulate and mobilise around causes that affect their immediate society. Through in-person meetings like townhalls and even protest marches they engage the people over unpopular policies. In Nigeria, such formal functional groups or social forces include the Nigerian Bar Association (NBA), Nigerian Labour Congress (NLC), Movement for the Survival of Ogoni People (MOSOP), the Academic Staff Union of Universities (ASUU) and a host of professional and socio-cultural unions. These and several others have contributed in no small measure to policy and governance in Nigeria. Political process in Nigeria therefore involves engagement with certain social forces.

SOCIAL FORCES AND CLIMATE ACTION IN NIGERIA

In the same light, the subject of climate change and Nigerian government's compliance with her multilateral agreements in this regard cannot be insulated from social forces. The forebearer to present day social forces in environment and climate change is traceable to the activism of the Movement for the Survival of the Ogoni People (MOSOP) that brought international attention to the plight of the people in the Niger Delta (Adeola, 2000). Since the discovery of oil in the mid-20th century, the region already had a history of ethnic minorities raising awareness about their plight due to the extractive activities of oil companies (Oluduro, 2015). Symbolized by Isaac Boro in the sixties, the intellectual dimension provided by Kenule Saro Wiwa in the eighties and nineties transformed MOSOP to a recognised social force in Nigeria. But the Koko waste dump disaster of 1987 remains the most scandalous environmental disaster in Nigeria that beamed global searchlight on the indiscriminate treatment of the environment in Nigeria and the Niger Delta in particular (Sampei & Aoyagi, 2009). In the sequence of events, a businessman from Italy Gianfrance Raffaelli imported toxic waste and dumped the drums of waste in Koko, Delta State. 20 out of 100 loaders of the drums died within a few months. The news of this opprobrious international act stirred national consciousness and rallied action on the environment.

According to Bob (2001;2002), in the face of global developments like the end of the Cold War and the increasing insistence by the European Community for minority rights to be respected against the background of the genocide in Yugoslavia, MOSOP appealed to transnational support for their campaign. Guided by Saro-Wiwa, the organization visited human rights organizations, Non-Governmental Organization and participated at several international conferences to build network. The Unrepresented Nations and Peoples Organization emerged as the main international supporter of the Ogoni cause (Osha, 2006). Apart from building international support for MOSOP, the UNPO also acted as a clearing house for her press releases. With the passage of time MOSOP also reframed her struggle beyond minority rights to embrace environmental issues (Bob, 2001; 2002). These attracted influential organizations like Greenpeace, and Amnesty International (Bob, 2001). We see here that with reframing, MOSOP shifted the narrative from ethnic minority rights which was more about political autonomy, to an environmental agenda (Bob, 2001). MOSOP's success in attracting big environmental non state actors to her cause shifted international focus to the activities of oil companies in Nigeria and the impact they have on the environment. This development attracted local attention by non-state actors to the environmental impact of industrial activity which was hitherto a purely state affair (Osha, 2006).

The above analogy is to demonstrate that social forces do not act alone. In fact, the most successful social forces enjoy transnational advocacy networks. In the twentieth century the nature of interactions most especially by non-state actors are structured within networks (Keck & Sikkink, 1998; 1999). These networks usually try to determine policy or change aspects of the global system to accommodate their values. MOSOP made effective use of these networks as the networks provide access to influence and resources. Such strategy is most useful when the domestic environment is not enabling the aspiration of a social force. By engaging transnational support, MOSOP utilized what Keck and Sikkink (1998; 1999) term 'boomerang effect'. This describes how groups in a country (A) appeal to citizens in another country (B) through a recognized entity abroad, to pressurize their home government (B) against the errant regime (A). For instance, in some other climes like the United Kingdom, the media is identified as a veritable tool that influences government's response to climate change (Harper & Philoa, 2013). In Nigeria, Non-governmental Organisations are seen in the same light as major forces leveraging pressure on government to comply with her UNFCCC agreements. For instance, the role of NGOs in drawing both local and international attention to the damage from oil spillage in the Niger Delta, led to an environmental impact assessment report by the United Nations Environmental Program (UNEP) of oil pollution in Ogoni land (Elenwo & Akankali, 2003). Since the breakthrough provided by MOSOP in the nineties, investors/financiers, multilateral financial institutions, civil society, communities, individuals, donor/development organisations, federal, state and local governments, private individuals, academics as well as Non Governmental Organisations, constitute the actors in climate change activities in Nigeria. These domestic stakeholders can be classified into three major groups viz: NGOs/CSO, Government Establishment/Public Sector and Private Corporations/Private Sector. These are also the social forces driving climate action in Nigeria.

CHAPTER FIVE

PUBLIC SECTOR AND INITIATIVES IN CLIMATE ACTION

GOVERNMENT IN CLIMATE ACTION

Government in Nigeria is a ubiquitous establishment and serves as the launchpad for most community-focused initiatives. On the subject of climate change, the public sector has taken some initiatives which would be presented in the following subsections. Since the return to democratic rule in 1999, the country has taken measures that presupposed and indicated her positive disposition to climate action.

A measure to improve her national capacity to generate observational climate change data and climate monitoring systems is the Department of Meteorological Services in the Ministry of Aviation which was upgraded to a full-fledged meteorological agency in 2003 - Nigeria Meteorological Agency (NiMET). This agency is tasked with the responsibility for climate research and observation.

There is also the commitment to cease gas flaring by harnessing environmentally friendly means of generating revenue within the gas industry. In this regard, the country has developed 2 gas reduction projects under the clean development mechanism. Four more are under validation. In fact, in 2012, 33.8% of CDM projects in Africa were located in Nigeria drawing from the deliberate efforts of the federal government through a gas capture and commercialization policy, to refine and deliver gas products which could otherwise be flared. As a result, only 8% of Nigeria's gas is currently flared (ICEED, 2019). These are concrete initiatives being pursued by government in response to the challenge of climate change.

It is germane to underscore that climate change is represented at the highest level of governance under the auspices of the Presidential Implementation Committee on Clean Development Mechanism (Hussein & Karaye, 2015). The following remarkable initiatives also stand out to enhance climate action in Nigeria.

NATIONAL ADAPTATION STRATEGY & PLAN OF ACTION (NASPA)

Government in cooperation with Civil Society Organisations prepared the national Adaptation Strategy and Plan of Action (NASPA) along with several experts. But integrating this into the country's overarching national development is still a challenge. This calls for a robust climate policy with clear cut direction for action (Ajao & Ogunniyi, 2009, 25).

It will be very interesting to see if the aimed integration of the National Adaptation Strategy process into national development planning and the increased multi-sectoral stakeholder inputs will help to manage and coordinate the different initiatives better. The need for more policy coordination and inclusion however has already been recognized by government: The elaboration of a comprehensive climate policy in order to consolidate all actions taken on climate change under one coordinating framework has been designated as most urgent post-COP15 project (Koblowsky & Speranza, 2010).

INTER-MINISTERIAL COMMITTEE ON CLIMATE CHANGE

This was established in 1993 just after the Rio Convention, to isolate and harmonise climate change matters in the country. The Ministries of Finance, Agriculture and Rural Development, Water Resources and Foreign Affairs, as well as Energy Commission of Nigeria, Nigeria National

Petroleum Corporation, National Planning Commission and the Nigeria Meteorological Agency currently represent government on the ICCC. There are representatives of NGOs and the Nigerian Environmental Study Action Team mainly from the academia with three special centres from the Federal University of Technology Minna's centre for climate change and fresh water resources; the Obafemi Awolowo University's centre for Energy research and development; and lastly resource persons from the Abubakar Tafawa Balewa University Bauchi, as the main repertoire for resource persons on climate change research (Hussein & Karaye, 2015).

After its creation, the work of the ICCC was coordinated by the Special Climate Change Unit (SCCU) which was upgraded to a full fledged department of climate change in 2011. Before its transformation, the SCCU introduced the National Climate Change Roundtable (NCCR) to engage all domestic stakeholders on one platform. Today, the department coordinates both the ICCC and the NCCR. Other responsibilities include inventory of GHG emissions and mitigation options, assessment of vulnerability, research on climate change science, publicity, act as designated authority for Clean Development Mechanism, participate at UNFCCC meetings, academic partnerships, collaboration with multilateral agencies and NGOs. It harmonises national, regional and international climate change projects and initiatives.

THE GREAT GREEN WALL AGENCY

The Great Green Wall Programme in Nigeria is part of the Great Green Wall for Sahel and Sahara Initiative (GGWSSI). GGWSSI was established by the African Union in 2007 with the objective to harmonize regional strategy to build climate change resilience in the Sahel and Sahara through effective management of ecosystems (Sani, 2018). The UN launched the same programme in 2008 under the United Nation Convention to Combat Desertification (UNCCD). This interconnected intervention which centered on planting of trees, was initiated to address the multiple challenges faced by people in the Sahel and Sahara. At the onset, the GGW project was conceived as a wall of trees from West Africa to East Africa before its evolution to a local integrated programme on climate change induced desertification. The programme is designed with a set of activities as part of the regional strategy on drought, land degradation and desertification. This includes political commitments by decision makers on good practices in rural development (Dilonardo, 2019). Based on the regional plan, the GGW is implemented by 20 countries on the continent of Africa with a budget of 8 million dollars.

Consequently, the GGW is "an integrated rural development programme to address the problem of environmental degradation in the sahel-sahara area and improve the livelihood of the affected communities (Sani, 2018, 29). The green wall is expected to stop vitiation or damage to land resources in the area. With the reversal of land degradation from climate vulnerability, it is expected that sustainable land management will lead to productivity and income among the rural populace. Under the GGW project, rural communities of West Africa especially, will collaborate in sustainable land management and food security. As national efforts are connected, barriers that intensify climate change, causing desertification and risks of conflict are checked.

Geographically, the GGW covers degraded and degrading land in the Sahel and Sahara with less than 400 millimeters of rainfall. Against the background of SDG Agenda 15.3 on the neutrality of degraded land by the year 2030, the GGW is pursued with the objective of restoring 10 million hectares annually in the area covering 780 million hectares. With the intervention of the GGW, it is expected that climate resilience will improve, carbon sequestration enhanced with built food security system and green jobs created leading to sustainable production and consumption. The wall foresees transformation of lives through the restoration of degraded landscape.

Nigeria is a party to the GGW project and established the National Agency for the Great Green Wall (NAGGW) with a five yearly strategic plan. The plan aims to reduce vulnerability to climate change induced desertification through land degradation. The improvement of land use and climate infrastructure is the major strategy to achieve this objective. As a development programme in Nigeria, the objective of the GGW is to protect ecosystems so as to promote sustainable livelihoods. It is foreseen that 22,500 square kilometers of Nigeria's dry region will be restored for agricultural production by 2030 and 25 million people will see improvement in their livelihood by the year 2030.

Thus, the GGW has enormous potential for food security, water stability, new economic opportunities and ultimately, combat climate change. This is crucial for sustainable development of dry lands most especially in the North-West and North-East region of Nigeria comprising eleven frontline states on the belt for the Great Green Wall; and occupying 43% of the country's landmass.

Besides the NAGGW, Nigeria has created other agencies to meet the challenges of climate change. This comprise the National Centre for Climate Change in Akure, Nigeria Institute for Marine Research in Lagos, National Institute of Freshwater Fisheries Research in New Bussa and the National Centre for Arid Zone Studies in Maiduguri.

It is important to state that with the collaboration of these agencies, Nigerian Government has formulated policies that promote climate action leading to the Nigerian environmental policy of 1999. Before that, there were National Effluent Limitation Regulation(1991), National Guidelines(standards) for environmental pollution control in Nigeria (1991), waste management regulations, pollution abatement in industries and facilities generating waste regulations (1991), environmental impact assessment decree Number 86 of 1992 and the National Resources conservation action plan (1999).

STATE GOVERNMENTS AND CLIMATE ACTION/INITIATIVES

Even though the initiatives of the federal government are the most visible with regards to climate action, some states in Nigeria have undertaken environmental reforms that affect climate action. These manifest as legislations or publicity programmes on environmental pollution or even land degradation.

For the oil-bearing states of the Niger Delta, ending gas flaring is a major challenge. In this connection, they have taken different approaches. Apart from engaging with local oil companies, they have forged international ties to drum support for this cause. Koblowsky & Speranza (2010) reveal that Rivers and Delta states consistently reach-out to American politicians to dissuade oil companies from gas flaring. Their research shows that following such demarche, Delta state announced that chevron oil promised to end the practice within two years from 2010.

Koblowsky & Speranza also inform of state governments' initiatives at sub-national levels. They commend the new coalition of sub national leaders formed to address problems in the environment. Hopefully, this will translate into funding for climate change responses. Lagos state government is leading the way as the first to develop a climate change policy. Evidence of the impact of that policy can be seen in the tree planting campaign and a dedicated day for tree planting yearly, by the department for parks and gardens. Other states like Kano, Kaduna, Enugu as well as the federal capital Abuja are initiating climate resilience strategies. In this category of states, Enugu state has a substantive resilience officer. All these point to the fact that the State governments see opportunities in low carbon economic growth. This role is also recognised by the national government and is being supported through cooperative actions (Koblosky & Speranza, 2010).

There are also evidences demonstrating that the national and state governments are gradually learning lessons in coordinating climate action. Nebo (2015) states that in ridding the country of ozone depleting substances, as a signatory to the Montreal Protocol (MP), Nigeria committed to putting in place measures that ensure that production and use of these ozone depleting substances that cause global warming are phased out (UNEP, 2015). Nebo's investigation reveals that in 2015 a hydrocarbon plant was built in Ogun state to produce refrigerants that have limited atmospheric impact. Going forward, more plants are encouraged nationwide.

Nebo (2015) also clarifies that in promoting sustainable environmental practices - with funding from the Global Environmental Facility (GEF), governments have continued to support the Pollution Department in reducing the emission or release into the environment of unintended persistent organic pollutants (UPOPs) which stay in the environment for years, destroying organic life. In Nigeria, these are widespread in form of accumulated wastes from homes and farms. But thanks to GEF, a lot of these wastes are recycled in some states. In Kano and Anambra states, waste from agriculture are recycled back to the farms. Industrial waste burning is also banned. Given the environmental benefits of these initiatives, other states – Ekiti, Rivers and Cross River are now adopting similar practice.

Thus, Nebo (2015) affirms governments' continuous zeal at integrating issues of climate, disaster risk and energy at both national and sub-national levels and focus on building resilience and ensuring that development remains risk informed and sustainable. He similarly opines that in the face of continuous unpredictable weather patterns, Nigeria has developed the Nigeria Agriculture Resilience Framework (NARF). Although not fully implemented, the NARF gives guidance to the country's path to climate smart agriculture; an approach to developing the technical, policy and investment conditions to achieve sustainable agricultural development for food security under climate change (Govind, Selvi & Karuppaiah, 2017). This entails; sustainably increasing agricultural productivity and incomes; adapting and building resilience to climate change as well as reducing and/ or removing greenhouse gases emissions. The policy is expected to give life to the country's existing National Climate Change Response Policy that will guide the implementation of future actions on climate change. It will guide all sectors towards achieving the goal of low carbon, high growth and resilient socio-economic systems for equitable socio-economic and environmental development (Nebo, 2015).

The above demonstrate that climate action can be streamlined into state policy as state governments in Nigeria are beginning to appreciate the progressive quality of climate action. These are happening as the opportunities in the blue economy and green technology are becoming more evident globally. But the negligible number of climate active states calls for more political awareness to galvanise widespread climate action. Underscoring the global nature of climate change entails that crafting a national or domestic policy will not be easy. But if state stakeholders are able to acknowledge the problems which are cross sectoral, a political solution will not be far in sight (Koblowsky & Speranza, 2010). In this context, there's need for a framework comprising all states to manage stakeholders' participation. With this, there will be more synergy, including incorporation of state-level initiatives.

CHAPTER SIX

NON-GOVERNMENTAL ORGANIZATIONS AND INITIATIVES IN CLIMATE ACTION

According to Koblosky and Speranza (2010) Nigeria's NGOs actively participate in climate governance. Infact, since 2015, the network of domestic climate actors has expanded exponentially. With the support of the NGOs, even the Nigerian media is advancing the dialogue on climate change issues in the country. With limited financial support from government, the media also relies on the NGOs for sponsorships and training to grasp the nuances of environmental problems, most especially climate change. In many cases, reports on climate change are either activities of the NGOs, NGO-sponsored feature stories on climate change adaptation or mitigation or news items stimulated by NGOs. Consequently, one can say that the disposition of the media on climate change in Nigeria is a reflection of the NGOs. Simply put, when it comes to climate change matters in Nigeria, supposedly separate groups like NGOs and media operate as one entity.

These climate related NGOs play significant role in public policy. They apply their position to guide institutions coordinating climate action (Koblowsky & Speranza, 2010). These include finetuning legislation to accommodate international concerns while addressing local problems. They also use this medium to engage official representatives and the public on climate change and climate action (Koblowsky & Speranza, 2010). All these demonstrate that NGOs are very active players in the country's climate action. For instance, the Henry Boll Foundation from Germany is prominent in her engagement with the department of climate change and other public sector departments. Her publications on the subject have served experts in climate change research and action even though the reports emphasize the need for mitigation action (Zirra, Usman & Modibbo, 2019). The coordinating role of the UNDP with the NGOs in the media significantly contribute to awareness creation and publicity in vulnerable communities about adaptation measures as a response to climate change. Nigeria's NDC document also buttresses the role of the NGOs by recognizing that "intermediate NGOs are critical in building community support for adaptation" (NDC, 2016, p.22). Being the most widespread climate-oriented body, the harnessing of NGOs is central to the success of climate action measures in Nigeria where public sector is still hamstrung by domestic and international commitments in several fields. But being the closest think-tank to both public sector and the international community, the NGOs are the most strategic to national adaptation response and should be harnessed and more coordinated (Koblowsky & Speranza, 2010). And bearing in mind the dearth of capacity on the part of public sector in optimally driving climate action, NGOs should be encouraged to continue energising the process.

CHAPTER SEVEN

PRIVATE SECTOR AND INITIATIVES IN CLIMATE ACTION

TWO PRIVATE SECTORS

In driving the climate change agenda in Nigeria, the country's private sector has been accused of detachment from the general conversation on climate change. It was only recently, after the COP15 conference, which was largely frequented by Nigerian businesses, that Nigeria's economic sector increasingly became active on the issue (Koblowsky & Speranza, 2010). From this moment, they advocated for a framework that will spur the business community. When it comes to climate change, it is important to make an important distinction between the oil and non-oil private sector. The multinational oil companies make up the oil industry or sector while the non-oil sector refers to general manufacturing, trade and services.

According to Ajao & Ogunniyi in Koblowsky and Speranza (2010), the oil industry in Nigeria is the most critical in determining public policy on the environment. It has many ties with government. Due to these ties, Koblowsky & Speranza insist that the industry in Nigeria is distinct from NGOs or the general private sector. The main expression of these ties is seen in joint venture entrepreneurship. Given the fact that oil is the mainstay of the country's economy, reaching 90% of Nigeria's foreign exchange, it is only natural that the clout of the oil industry will be enormous (Koblowsky & Speranza, 2010).

The nature of this relationship entails that interests between government and the oil companies consistently overlap. Based on these binary interests, the oil companies have representatives in many government boards including establishments that are climate related (Koblowsky & Speranza, 2010). These authors reveal that oil companies are present in the National Committee on Climate Change and provision will most likely be made for their representatives in the upcoming National Commission on Climate Change. With this level of influence, the oil industry is able to control the narrative on environmental impact (Amadi, 2008). This is reflected in the popular advocacy for adaptation measures to build resilience against environmental impact. This may not be unconnected with the fact that the many environmental problems are caused by oil exploration. Unfortunately, the non oil private sector and NGOs cannot match the oil industry in their influence to control the narrative.

But the fact remains that it is still a challenge for multinational petroleum corporations in Nigeria to totally abandon gas flaring with new technology. And it has been difficult for the government to coerce enforcement, thus demonstrating the oil sector's influence on national climate policy (Koblowsky & Speranza, 2010). Okorodudu- Fubara (2001) even states that the oil sector's political influence delayed Nigeria's long-standing non-ratification of the Kyoto Protocol. What this means is that, if the oil industry transits to clean energy, it will have a domino effect on national policy and other sectors of the economy.

It is clear therefore that in these two private sectors schema in Nigeria's climate action, the oil industry controls more capital and influence in both the society and government. Thus they constitute a unique and more formidable social force. With sufficient capital they can suppress their abuses and magnify their isolated initiatives on climate action. As a bloc, they also have external collaborators like OPEC as well as other multinational corporations. These advantages further improve their impetus in the eyes of a government that seeks assistance in many forms from them. In the end, this oil-based private sector is able to influence public policy in their favour. They are also able to get away with infractions that have bearings on climate change.

Unfortunately, this is not the case for the non-oil private sector which is faced with the problem of capital from the onset. These private companies find it difficult to operate in a new business environment like renewable energy that is capital intensive. The situation is further worsened by the country's weak technological base to support their efforts (Olawuyi, 2017). With the odds stacked against the non-oil private sector, any hope on them to drive climate action against the current of the oil industry has little chance of being realized. It is for this reason that the activities of the private sector in climate action has remained low. Poor finance and technology have affected their capacity in many respects including partnership with government. Meanwhile, the enabling of this social force as a single entity is the key to significant climate action by Nigeria. This therefore calls for a situation where research, government, industry and NGOs make conscious efforts to strengthen the private sector in climate action.

CHAPTER EIGHT

ANALYSES OF DOMESTIC STAKEHOLDERS' ASSESSMENT OF ADAPTATION AND MITIGATION

For better insight on domestic stakeholders' action, it is important to elicit the opinion and reaction of some social forces who are directly involved in climate action in the country. In this connection, I refer here to a select random survey of domestic climate stakeholders conducted in 2019. The outcome of the study involving 384 respondents (derived using Cochran's sampling guidelines for indefinite population), is very relevant in our analyses of the scenario of adaptation and mitigation action in Nigeria. On this ground, a large part of the quantitative data in this chapter is drawn from the survey, whose questions are affixed as appendices to this text. As a limitation, this survey is not fully representative of the gamut of climate actors in the country. Nevertheless, its outcome most likely resonates with other stakeholders for the period under review.

ANALYSING NIGERIA'S ADAPTATION ACTION

From the survey, the following initiatives were acknowledged as significant adaptation measures: capacity building training for few government officials and NGO staff, durable housing in rural areas, more cooperation with NGOs and the need to build resilience in communities, more environmental reports and sponsored Media programs on environment like Green Angle (TVC), ECO-Africa (Channels TV), initiation of climate friendly policies like National Adaptation Strategy and Plan of

Action, National Climate Change Response Policy, National Agency for the Green Wall Initiative, better drainage systems in urban areas, improved seedlings and mixed cropping, development of alternative occupation or skills in rural areas to supplement livelihood. In spite of these, the respondents rated Nigeria "very poor" in adaptation. This also corresponded overwhelmingly with the feedback on question three where majority of the respondents strongly agreed that Nigeria's environmental needs mentioned above affected her ability to comply with the UNFCCC agreements. In essence, the absence of existing environmental protective measures in many localities affected the ability to adapt to climate change. Consequently, their environmental needs affected compliance. Thus, majority of the respondents in the survey and the interview gave a poor assessment of Nigeria in terms of adaptation.

The above rating by stakeholders necessitates the need to provide clarity on Nigeria's adaptation measures. In this regard, the SNC attests that adaptation intiatives resulted in the reduction of many human casualties as a consequence of disaster. Adoption of irrigation farming practices for instance in the arid zones in the north of the country under the FADAMA farming programme by the state and federal governments stands out as successful examples. Feedbacks from interviewees corroborated the claims in some literature that among other inventions, researchers have also been able to produce efficient cooking methods that reduce pressure on forest wood (Oladipo, 2010). The survey also identified adaptive measures in Nigeria. The country's NDC further indicates that, government's assistance in the conversion of rural shelter from clay-thatched houses to burnt bricks with corrugated roofing sheets have also emerged as resilient means of adaptation (NDC, 2016). Along the coastlines, the construction of dykes to reduce the impact of climate change from sea level rise was also developed. All these are concrete adaptation measures. But unfortunately, these initiatives are isolated and are far between; and as such, cannot suffice to ensure effective compliance with the UNFCCC by Nigeria in the area of adaptation.

The above problem in terms of adaptation in Nigeria is complicated by the absence of comprehensive records of such measures around the country. This is in agreement with the observation of respondents that in a federal system of government where the central government has little or no control on the subsidiary state governments' activities on climate change, computing such information is a problem. And central to this problem is the issue of capacity at the local level, which is worse than that at the Centre. It was observed that in the interim, there was the lack of interest on climate change issues. One sentiment was that climate action did not attract immediate economic benefits to the provincial coffers. This gravely affected capacity building in that area. Owing to lack of interest, records of adaptation measures were not consciously taken for policy and planning purposes at the local level and the high cost of adaptation initiatives, which cannot be offset by existing funds at the state level, were neither systematically collected nor computed, but rather avoided.

ANALYSING NIGERIA'S MITIGATION ACTION

From the survey, we saw that even though in terms of mitigation Nigeria had taken measures like reduction in gas flaring, increased utilization of gas for energy production, improved solar energy utilization, engagement with foreign partners on the possibility for renewable technology transfer as well as a proposed climate change bill, most of the respondents rated Nigeria very poor here too. The responses to question seven illustrated a "poor" assessment of Nigeria in terms of mitigation by majority of the stakeholders. In the same vein, under question 13, 51% of the stakeholders "strongly agreed" with Nigeria's compliance level while 7% "disagreed."

In general, feedback from the interviewees vehemently provided a negative assessment of Nigeria's compliance with the UNFCCC agreements. This negative assessment of Nigeria's compliance is further complicated by inadequate records to measure Nigeria's quantitative or scaled compliance as reflected in the NDC (NDC, 2016). As such, support from outside would be needed to remedy the problem. Nigeria's NDC reiterates this fact when it states that, "we are committed to developing a monitoring, reporting and verification (MRV) system with support from international partners" (NDC, 2016, p.17). In this regard, the country in her communication to the UNFCCC only promises to cut down emission by 20% in the first commitment period if supported by developed countries. From the illustration in Nigeria's NDC below (Fig. 8.1), it is clear that in the past, the support from the developed countries was insignificant with Nigeria requiring about 80 million tonnes of oil with its accompanying emissions as energy demand. And if business proceeds as usual as had been the case in the past, the country is expected to require more than 180 million tonnes of oil by 2030 when states are expected to reduce their emissions to less than 1.5^c by 2030. This calls for more aggressive measures to remedy the situation.

Looking at the submission in the FNC, SNC and NDC above, we see a great correlation with the problems and solutions evoked in the responses to questions 14 and 15 in the feedback from the stakeholders. The graphs and tables from official documents (FNC, SNC, NDC, and NASPA) provide further details below.

Figure 8.1: Energy Demand – Business As Usual Versus Efficient Green Scenarios

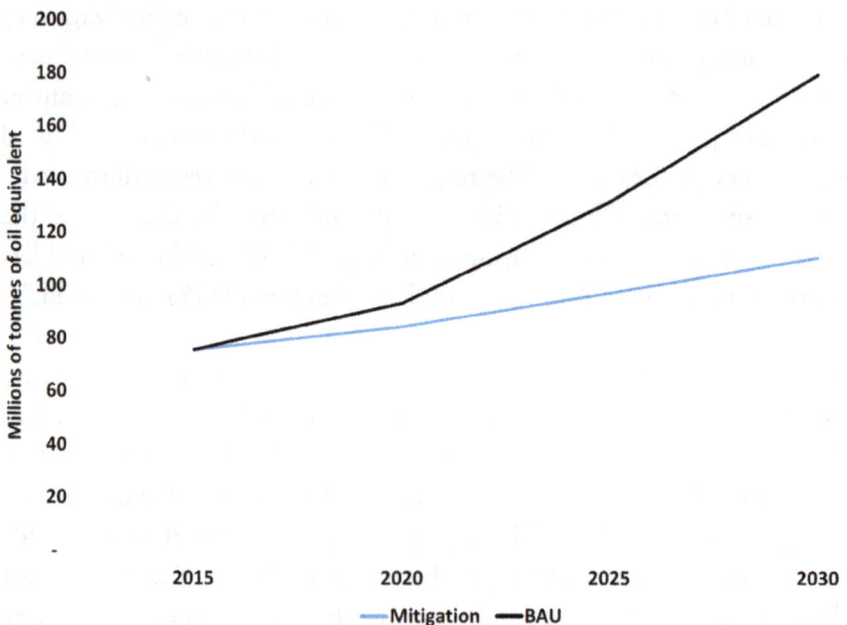

Source: *NDC (2016)*

But in terms of carbon emission, figure 8.2 vividly illustrates the projection for Nigeria for the past, present and the future. We see that as of 2010, over 300 million tonnes of carbondioxide equivalent was emitted and this has increased progressively over the years to over 400 million tonnes of carbondioxide equivalent emissions by 2015 and 2016 respectively. From this submission by the Nigerian designated authorities on climate change which is the department of climate change, this scenario is bound to increase if nothing is done about it (business as Usual), to over a billion tonnes of emission in 2030. From this report, even with the right political will, emission will still reach 700 million tonnes in 2030. This goes to prove that the only way for emission to reduce significantly in future is with the assistance of developed countries at 400 million tonnes. This gives a difference of 600 million tonnes between external help and being left to respond within her limited capacity.

Figure 8.2: Mitigation Action

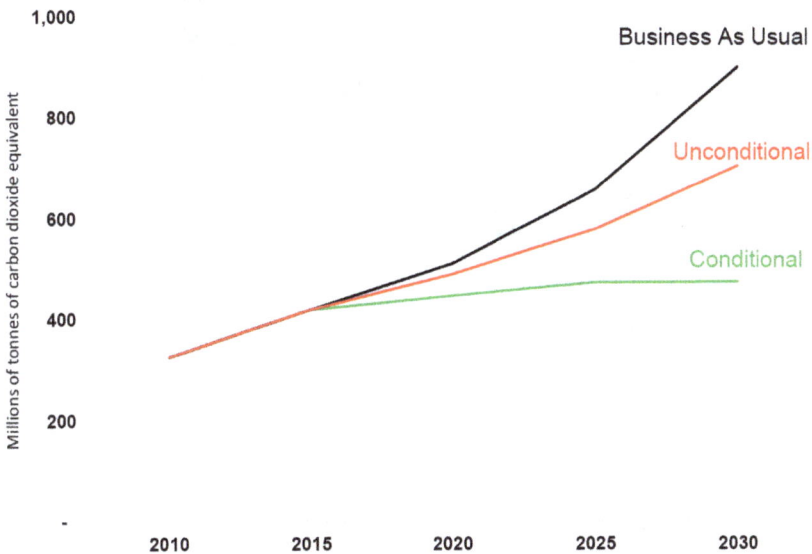

Source: NDC (2016)

Table 8.1: Emission from Nigeria (1850-2010)

Information	Value	Source
Historical emissions (1850-2010)	2,564.02 million tonnes (MT)	CAIT database, World Resources Institute
1990 emissions	163.91 MT	Nigeria's Second National Communication
2000 emissions	214.21 MT	Nigeria's Second National Communication
2010 emissions	263.0 MT	Energy Commission of Nigeria

Source: (NDC, 2016)

Figure 8.3: Source of 2030 Emission Reduction by Sector

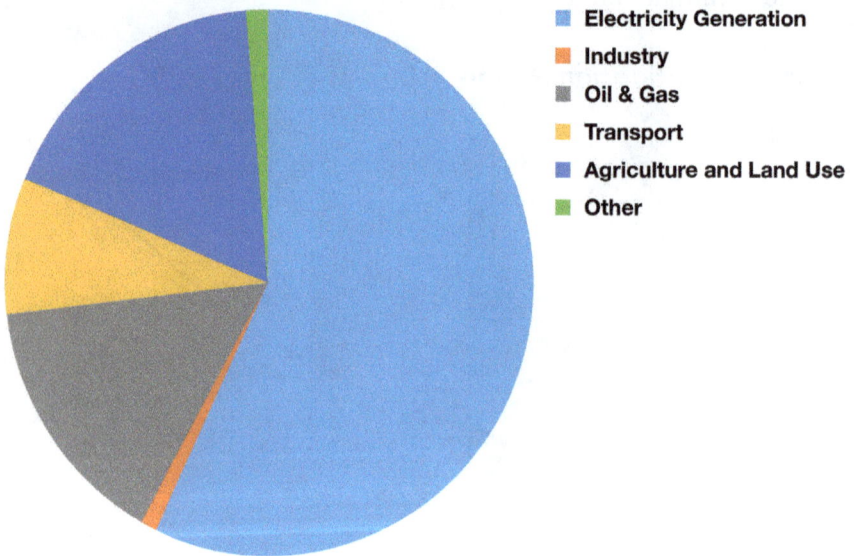

Source: NDC (2016)

It should however be noted that though the country has shown compliance in submitting reports (FNC,SNC, NDC) with the assistance of expertise from the UNFCCC secretariat, these reports agree that there have been challenges with regard to implementing the voluntary commitments by Nigeria. In fig 8.3 above, we see that the major area of emission reduction will be in the area of electricity generation which is commendable. By this projection, Nigeria is expected to have more stable power supply by 2030, presumably from solar energy and gas. This will drastically reduce emission from power generating sets which according to statements from one of this study's interviewee from the private sector, "about 3.5 trillion naira is spent on generator fuel annually." This is a huge burden on household and industries running on non-renewable or perishable energy. Cutting emission from fuel emission is most commendable bearing in mind that Nigeria's main area of emission is in the area of energy. With 58% of energy derived from renewable energy the country would be on the path to clean energy development.

But again, the chart indicates that heavy areas of current emission will not see significant change by the SDG target year 2030. Sectors like industry will only reduce emission by 2%, Oil and Gas sector by 15%, transport 10% and Agriculture 12%. These figures go to prove that the areas of emission reduction in electricity generation will not affect critical sectors of the economy. Only household electricity will be the major area of emission reduction for electricity generation.

As a leading exporter of crude oil, Nigeria also refines the substance for domestic use, resulting in the indiscriminate flaring of the associated gases with its attendant impact on global climate change (Ogbodo & Ngozi, 2014). In fact, since Nigeria started oil production in commercial quantity in 1956, gas has been flared into the atmosphere, despite the environmental consequences. But within the timeframe of our study, the amount of gas flared reduced drastically. In table 8.1, record of gas flared by companies were collected and collated by industrial actors. The record from the Nigerian National Petroleum Corporation (NNPC) indicates that capacity for utililisation of gas was improved upon, resulting in reduction in gas flaring.

It is however germane to observe here that even though gas flaring drastically reduced between 2000 and 2016 as indicated in table 8.2, it is still far below what was projected in the first national communication in fig. 8.4 below. By that projection, Nigeria should only be emitting barely 120 petajourles of flared gas by 2010. On the contrary, the country flared about 24% of its gas production in 2010 with higher emission rates until when it dropped from 2012 to 2017 at 12.33% of gas flared (Table 8.2). It is instructive to highlight the observation by the interviewee from the public sector informing that improved use of gas power stations for electricity was responsible for the improvement in gas utilization in the country leading to reduction in gas flaring. As such, we see in table 8.3 that in recent global rating, Nigeria and Algeria shifted places in global gas flaring with Algeria now the major emitter on the continent. This is because of the gas flare recovery project of the Nigerian government (Ati, Agubamah & Abaje, 2018). This goes to demonstrate that ending gas flaring in Nigeria is possible before the deadline of "zero routine flaring by 2030" launched by former UN Secretary General Ban Ki-Moon on April 17, 2015 and endorsed by Governments and oil companies including Nigeria (World Bank, 2016). Before now, Nigeria flared 400 million tons of carbon into its environment. 25 million cubic feet of gas was flared daily, totaling 40% of the continent's gas consumption. This was one sixth of global gas emission. From table 8.2 from NNPC, this has improved in the last six years. The federal government achieved this feat through its gas recovery project as well as the Nigerian Gas Flare Commercialization Programme (NGCP) targeted at the 144 gas flaring points nationwide (Amaza, 2018). This has reinvigorated use of gas-power and industrialization which was unachievable under the Associated Gas Reinvigoration Act of 1980.

But it is unfortunate to still see gas being flared with the huge potentials for its use as compressed or liquefied product for energy use. As the leading exporter of crude oil in Africa with the highest gas deposit, Nigeria is supposed to lead in gas utilization.

It is somewhat ironical that despite the environmental and economic consequences of gas flaring, the country has not stopped the practice. From 1984, the initial deadline was extended to 2004, to 2007, 2008, 2010, 2012 and 2018. Yet, gas is still flared within Nigeria long after concerns by scholars (see Koblowsky & Speranza, 2010).

Table 8.2: Gas Produced, Utilized and Flared in Nigeria

Year	Gas Produced (mscf)	Gas Utilised (mscf)	Gas Flared (mscf)	% Flared
2000				
2001	5,208,348,890.00	25,771,898.30	29,311,590.60	0.51
2002	47,188,328.20	25,928,089.60	21,260,229.60	0.45
2003	52,230,894.00	28,072,561.20	24,158,332.80	0.46
2004	59,493,808.40	34,177,561.20	25,316,301.60	0.43
2005	57,861,127.90	34,744,142.70	23,116,988.30	0.40
2006	2,182,432,084.00	1,378,770,261.00		31.82
2007	2,415,649,041.00	1,655,960,318.00	759,688,726.00	31.45
2008	2,287,547,344.00	1,668,148,489.00	619,398,854.00	27.08
2009	1,837,278,307.00	1,327,926,402.00	509,351,908.00	27.72
2010	2,392,838,898.00	1,811,270,548.00	581,568,354.00	24.30
2011	2,400,402,880.00	1,781,370,022.00	619,032,858.00	28.79
2012	2,580,165,626.00	1,991,498,902.00	588,666,724.00	22.82
2013	2,325,137,449.00	1,916,531,001.00	409,311,430.00	17.60
2014	2,485,645,730.00	2,199,884,130.00	285,761,600.00	11.50
2015	2,929,852,323.00	2,588,480,059.00	341,372,264.00	11.65
2016	2,777,791,236.00	2,465,323,180.00	312,468,060.00	11.25
2017	2,901,632,487.00	2,543,928,718.00	357,703,770.00	12.33

Source: Nigerian National Petroleum Corporation (2018)

Figure 8.4. Projected Gas Produced and Utilised

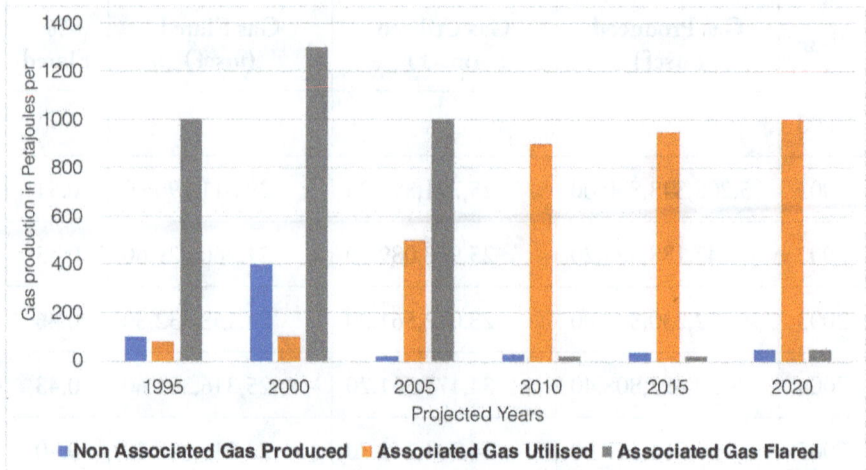

Source: Adapted from First National Communication (2003)

Table 8.3: Gas Flaring Data 2013-2017 (Billion Cubic Meters)

No.	Country	2013 bcm	2014 bcm	2015 bcm	2016 bcm	2017 bcm	2016-2017 change bcm	2013-2017 change bcm
1	Russia	19.9	18.3	19.6	22.4	19.9	-2.5	0.0
2	Iraq	13.3	14.0	16.2	17.7	17.8	0.1	4.6
3	Iran	11.1	12.2	12.1	16.4	17.7	1.3	6.6
4	United States	9.2	11.3	11.9	8.9	9.5	0.6	0.3
5	Algeria	8.2	8.7	9.1	9.1	8.8	-0.3	0.6
6	Nigeria	9.3	8.4	7.7	7.3	7.6	0.3	-1.7
7	Venezuela	9.3	10.0	9.3	9.3	7.0	-2.4	-2.3
8	Libya	4.1	2.9	2.6	2.4	3.9	1.6	-0.2
9	Angola	3.2	3.5	4.2	4.5	3.8	-0.7	0.6
10	Mexico	4.3	4.9	5.0	4.8	3.8	-1.0	-0.5
11	Malaysia	2.8	3.4	3.7	3.2	2.8	-0.3	0.0
12	Oman	2.4	2.6	2.4	2.8	2.6	-0.2	0.2
13	Kazakhstan	3.8	3.9	3.7	2.7	2.4	-0.2	-1.3
14	Egypt	2.4	2.8	2.8	2.8	2.3	-0.5	0.0

15	Indonesia	3.1	3.1	2.9	2.8	2.3	-0.4	-0.8
16	Saudi Arabia	2.0	1.9	2.2	2.4	2.3	-0.1	0.3
17	Turkmenistan	2.3	2.0	1.8	1.8	1.7	-0.2	-0.6
18	China	1.9	2.1	2.1	2.0	1.6	-0.4	-0.4
19	Gabon	1.4	1.5	1.6	1.6	1.5	-0.1	-0.1
20	India	1.7	1.9	2.2	2.1	1.5	-0.6	-0.2
21	United Kingdom	1.4	1.3	1.3	1.3	1.4	0.0	0.0
22	Canada	1.5	2.1	1.8	1.3	1.3	0.0	-0.2
23	Syria	0.4	0.4	0.5	0.6	1.2	0.6	0.8
24	Rep. of Congo	1.4	1.3	1.2	1.1	1.1	0.0	-0.3
25	Brazil	1.3	1.5	1.3	1.4	1.1	-0.3	-0.2
26	Ecuador	0.8	1.0	1.1	1.2	1.1	-0.1	0.3
27	Cameroon	0.8	0.9	1.1	1.1	1.0	-0.1	0.2
28	Qatar	1.4	1.3	1.1	1.1	1.0	0.0	-0.4
29	Vietnam	1.1	1.1	1.0	0.9	1.0	0.1	-0.1
30	UAE	1.2	0.9	1.0	0.8	1.0	0.1	-0.3
	Rest of world	12.5	12.8	11.1	10.0	8.4	-1.6	-4.0
	Global total	139.6	143.9	145.6	147.6	140.6	-7.1	1.0
	Source: NOAA, GGFR. Rounded Numbers							

Source: World Bank (2016)

In addition to gas flaring, persistent emission from transportation is another leading source of carbon emission. Furthermore, burning fossil fuels such as coal, petrol and oils for both domestic and commercial use contribute to Nigeria's climate change emission footprint (Ogbodo & Ngozi 2014).

In sum, Nigeria overwhelmingly depends on fossil fuel not just for revenue but for domestic uses. It is the predominant source of energy in homes, offices, industries and power plants. Central to the problem is that switching from fossil fuel to energy efficient method is capital intensive and may not be readily affordable due to poor infrastructure. The other problem is that, in a bid to accelerate development, Nigeria has consistently harnessed resources regardless of the consequences to the environment, health and social stability of her people. Unavoidable development is pursued recklessly against the balance of sustainability. There's even the attempt by pro-emission scholars to justify this alarming record that the size of a state's economy roughly correlates with its carbondioxide emission. Advocates of this position argue that Nigeria's 500 billion dollars economic base is a necessary outcome of high emission. Even though this is the case in Africa, several scenarios around the world point to the contrary. China for instance is not the biggest economy but remains the leading emitter for over a decade. Similarly, countries in the European Union with massive economy-scale, demonstrate low carbon footprint. Thus, the argument is unsustainable. It is on account of this environmental economic debate that Rudrappan (2011) condemns carbon-based development model as the error of neo-liberal theory of economic development where environmental growth is overlooked in the pursuit of development. The focus in the neo-liberal model is on income and energy consumption. Here the issue of income and biophysical growth is erroneously set aside which has been responsible for accelerated climate change. He argues that this market driven development which promotes liberalisation, privatisation and globalisation ultimately leads to only growth from foreign direct investment. It does not lead to broad-based industrial growth from endogenous capacity. Rather, the biggest beneficiaries of this carbon-based development are the transnational and multinational corporations and foreign investors who "enjoy tax holidays and non-insistence on environmental conditionality" (Rudrappan, 2011, p10). On the other hand, the victims are the domestic manufacturers and the people who are left to face the impact of environmental exploitation. Thus, in the long run, developing countries like Nigeria will be stuck at the receiving end. In his analysis of this neo-liberal development model, Rudrappan is of the opinion that given the catastrophic turn out of things, this old model's insistence on comparative advantage in foreign trade rather than agricultural diversity as well as low wage in manufacturing, are not conducive for developing countries. So in the end, the "big economy - big emitter" argument does not help the Nigerian cause. Rather these calls for the hard and difficult path to diversify the economy by embracing clean energy for production against the current one that is fossil-fuelled. Even the advocacy by neo-classical environmentalist that carbon based development should be permissible at the inception of development, since it will naturally drop as development progresses is described as "false assurance". The new thinking presupposes that, carbon neutral development is more of a rational decision than an economic necessity. The caveat here is that the earth is on a perilous path to extinction from carbon-based development and developing countries are the most vulnerable. The solution here as advocated by Rudrappan, is a carbon neutral development path.

As indicated by Nigeria's first and second communication, the major challenge for Nigeria to take mitigation action is in the area of energy production. Without addressing this problems, the setback to the country's compliance with her voluntary commitments under the UNFCCC will subsist for long.

Nigeria's mitigation action is also hampered by excessive deforestation. There is wood demand for logging, fuel, timber exports and agriculture. Between 2000 and 2005 for instance, the country cleared 58.7% of its forest.

Table 8.4: Forest as Percentage of Land Cover in Nigeria

Year	Land cover (Sq. km)	Year	Land cover (Sq. km)
1990	18.92245	2003	13.07487
1991	18.47261	2004	12.62514
1992	18.02277	2005	12.17541
1993	17.57293	2006	11.72568
1994	17.1231	2007	11.27595
1995	16.67325	2008	10.82622
1996	16.22342	2009	10.37649
1997	18.77358	2010	9.926765
1998	18.32374	2011	9.477036
1999	14.8739	2012	9.027307
2000	14.42406	2013	8.577578
2001	13.97433	2014	8.127848
2002	13.5246	2015	7.678119

Source: World Bank (2017)

Figure 8.5: Contribution of Charcoal to Total Deforestation

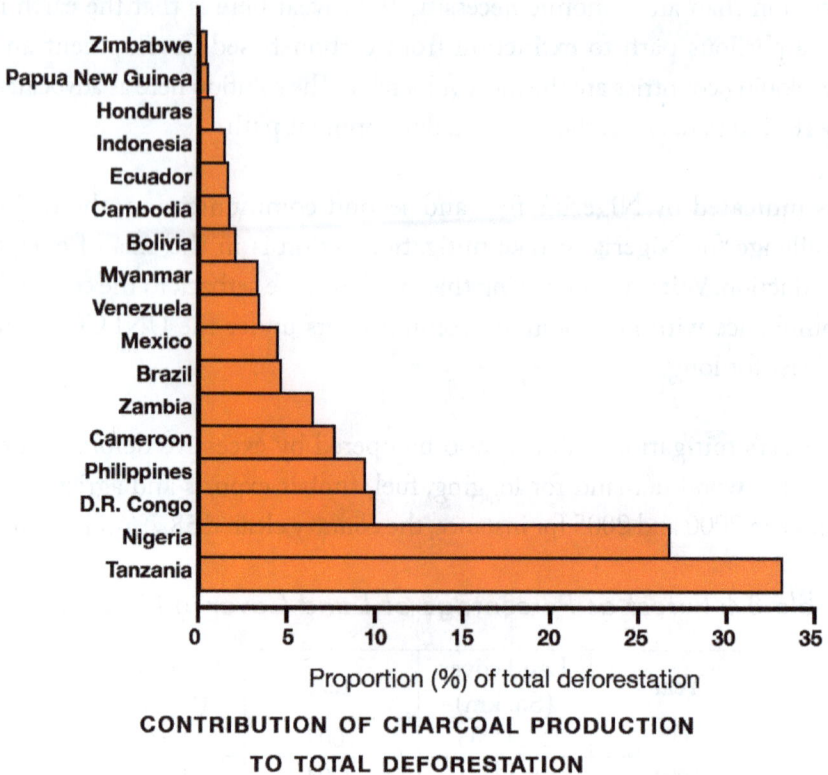

Proportion (%) of total deforestation

**CONTRIBUTION OF CHARCOAL PRODUCTION
TO TOTAL DEFORESTATION**

Source: SNC (2014)

These forest trees are formidable carbondioxide mitigants as they absorb the substance through photosynthesis. But hewing trees for economic and domestic ends weaken the atmosphere of this major bulwark to mitigate the environmental effect of carbondioxide. In figure 8.5 above, we see that Nigeria is only second to Tanzania in deforestation from charcoal production. Added to the menace of gas flaring, this development clearly portrays Nigeria's laxity in addressing environmental challenges that relate to climate change. Between 2000 and 2013 the country lost 79% of its forests (Batta, Ashong & Bashir, 2013). Today it is losing 11% annually. In monetary terms, six billion dollars is lost to deforestation against the background of arbitrary concessions. In terms of impact, 11 states are affected with annual loss of 8.4 billion dollars to drought and desert encroachment (Batta, Ashong & Bashir, 2013). The country is faced with southward desertification at 6%

annually, losing 350,000 hectares which reverses the gains of the great green wall. For emphasis, deforestation occurs at 4000 square kilometres annually while reforestation is 10 kilometres annually.

Even in Africa, the country is not in the category of countries showing leadership in arresting the destruction of the ecosystem. In advancing this position, reference is made to the "global land rush" where farmers are deprived of arable land to foreign investors principally for construction of highways and industrial sites (World Bank, 2010). Only 9.9% of Nigeria's land is protected forest. This is barely 9.1 square kilometres of its total landmass. To make matters worse, only 4% of tropical rainforest is untouched (Dada, Jibrin & Ijeoma, 2006). As these forests are replaced with large scale farming, the threat of climate change continues to intensify. Sadly, efforts by environmental activists to reverse these trends are coercely countered by governments at various levels (Mersha, 2009). The most visible evidence of such encroachment is in cross river state which hosts the largest vestiges of forest lands in Nigeria. In Zirra (p.169, 2019), an interviewee from the NGOs disclosed that,

> The government has embarked on the construction of a superhighway connecting the state to the middle belt region of the country with the objective of opening up the state for development and foreign investment. The consequence of the above is that, deprived forest dependent natives turn to environmentally harmful means of survival that includes fuel-wood vending, charcoal burning, encroachment on forest and ecological zones which have accompanying impact on climate change.

This destruction of forest cover surface was a major concern for respondents during the survey in 2019. This was against the background that, as the federal government expended resources elsewhere on the great green wall, a state government destroyed trees at the other end. But following intensive pressure from environmental stakeholders, the proposed destruction was averted. The scenario in cross river state poetically mirrors the situation in many, if not all developing countries; where governments are in dilemma over the choice between carbon neutrality and rapid industrialization. Just a few years back in 2011, Cross River state was commended as the only Nigerian state that showed commitment to UNFCCC agreement on Reduction of Emissions from Deforestation and Degradation (REDD) (Rudrappan, 2011). The recent development however, raises doubts over the state's political commitment to her official position on the promotion of biodiversity.

Thus, Nigeria's voluntary commitment to substantially reduce or mitigate GHG emissions is constrained. Key data on table 8.1 show that Nigeria's emission has increased geometrically between 1850-2010 (NDC, 2016). Data from world resource institute show that only 2,563.02 million tonnes of carbondioxide equivalent emission were recorded for Nigeria in 1850. But by 2010, Nigeria's emissions graduated to 263.0 million tonnes. Juxtaposing this with the data on fig 8.2 above, we see that emission continued unabated into 2016 with worse case scenarios for 2030. It is for this reason that the country will need developed countries to come to her assistance in her voluntary mitigation commitments. In the meantime, the interventions by developed countries have not been significant. This is despite the NNPC's efforts at reducing gas flaring in the last decade.

The foregone premises go to suggest that there are more cases of Nigeria's noncompliance than compliance with the UNFCCC in both adaptation and mitigation. Even though we have demonstrated that government and NGOs have initiated remarkable climate action, we must also acknowledge that these still fall below the UNFCCC expectations; as there are still many areas calling for climate action. In the same vein, drawing from the integrated analysis above, we can conclude that Nigeria's climate actions are shaped by environmental stakeholders led by NGOs and government establishments as the main drivers.

From the aggregate of opinion on question three, the respondents and interviewees concurred that social forces drive climate action in Nigeria, both to a "large extent" and a "very large extent." NGOs, Media, Government Officials, unions of host community, international organizations and the private sector were identified as the social actors driving climate change in Nigeria. In general, these tally with the classification of the ShE by the

UNFCCC. The private sector is identified as the least active social force in climate action in Nigeria. Even the questionnaire responses and interview feedback for this study showed low response of the private sector (14%), while the NGO (44%) and Government agencies (40%) dominate the number of respondents. In essence, NGOs followed by government are the major drivers of climate action in Nigeria.

SYNTHESISING THE SCENARIO ON CLIMATE CHANGE COMPLIANCE IN NIGERIA

In line with the convention's reporting mandate for all parties to regularly communicate the status of climate change in their jurisdiction (Art. 4), Nigeria submitted two national communications to the UNFCCC (FNC, 2003; SNC, 2014). In the First National Communication in 2003, which presented the country's gross national emissions of GHG, it reports that "gas flaring, transportation and electricity generation are the most significant energy consumption processes leading to GHG emissions" (FNC, 2003, p.5).

In terms of mitigation, the report indicates that GHG emission is generally based on per capita, but this will rise with population and resource consumption.

Noting the centrality of adaptation for developing countries under the UNFCCC, the report indicates the urgency for adaptation as rainfall in Nigeria is essential for livestock production involving more than 12 million cattle, 24 million goats and 8 million sheep raised principally in the northern states (FNC, 2003, p.8). In connection with rainfall, temperature rise in marine and freshwater will negatively affect fisheries and saltwater intrusion as well as destroy inland fisheries in rivers and lakes.

The Second National Communication (SNC) transmitted in 2014 is more elaborate. Overall, it states that the energy sector accounts for 70%, of GHG emissions followed by agriculture with 27% of emissions.

The SNC portrays Nigeria as a low-income developing country with under-utilized productivity and an oil dominant economy. Based on the report, energy is central to Nigeria's high GHG emission. In the energy subsector, oil is 53%, natural gas 39% and hydroelectricity 7%. Save for biomass used in rural cooking needs and heating, coal, nuclear energy and other renewables are not incorporated in Nigeria's energy consumption. In general, the SNC provides a comprehensive profile of climate change in Nigeria; clearly stating the country's socio-economic profile and environmental challenges. It even encourages adoption of low carbon procedures in the service sector to strengthen the economy.

Nigeria also submitted its Nationally Determined Contribution to UNFCCC in 2016. The document stipulates Nigeria's voluntary commitments regarding climate action with the signing and ratification of the Paris agreement. The projection is that by 2030, Nigeria should halve its emissions.

Unfortunately, the two development strategy documents since the return to civil rule only indicate passing interest in climate change. The vision 2020 under President Olusegun Obasanjo (1999-2007) "recognises climate change as a threat to sustainable growth in the next decade" (NDC, 2016, p.4). The document emphasises the threat to infrastructure, food, water and natural resource conflict. Owing to these, it calls for definite adaptation strategy and plan of action. Sadly, it did not devise any strategy nor take concrete steps in this regard. The year 2020 arrived and by then the threat and damage of climate change had intensified. Some scholars have lamented that the Transformation Agenda of Presidents Yar' Adua/Goodluck Jonathan (2007-2015) with 2011-2015 as its timeframe laid little emphasis on climate change. Generally, the policy and its implementation plan failed to attend to climate change as an area of priority. But the administration of Goodluck Jonathan that succeeded Yar' Adua tried to make up in its climate action by adopting the Nigeria Climate Change Response and Strategy in 2012. The objective here was to attain climate-proof economic growth and development. Using the post-mortem report of the 2012 Post-Disaster Need Assessment Report, the NDC warned that Nigeria would lose 2-11% of its GDP by 2020. In the report, the damage from flood in 2002 amounted to $16.9 billion representing 1.4% of GDP for that year only. After 2015, with her assent to the Paris Agreement, the country proclaimed its commitment to emission reduction as well as adaptation initiatives with a view to operate a clean energy regime (NDC, 2016). Cognizant of these, the NDC of 2016 states measures to transform the situation and increase the country's adaptation and mitigation measures. In the case of adaptation which should be Nigeria's focus as a developing country, the NDC document underlines Nigeria's lack of in-depth quantitative data on the cost of climate change.

Nebo (2015) observes that Nigeria lacks a substantive renewable energy or efficacy policy even though this is supposed to be a priority. What is meant here is that, Nigeria's energy policies were yet to become laws. After all, Nebo (2015) himself acknowledges the presidential approval of the Renewable Energy and Energy Efficacy Policy (REEP) with accompanying action plans – National Renewable Energy Action Plan (NREAP) and National Energy Efficiency Action Plan (NEEAP). Clearly, these policy and plans when fully operational will create the enabling environment for the energy sector to thrive. Meanwhile as of 2015, the demand for energy reached 30,000 mw. With the enormous shortfall in supply and demand, meeting the target of 40,000 mw by 2020 was unachievable. But again, following through with these commitments did not match the fervour with which it was announced. For instance, various committees were set up to carryout widespread reforms in the power sector. This was supposed to stimulate significant private sector participation with a credit line of $500 million. Unfortunately, in terms of climate action, there was no significant manifestation between 2002 and 2015 which comprised the lifespan of the Obasanjo and Yar Adua/Jonathan regimes. This however is not to imply that nothing was done. But these were insignificant compared to the country's limitless potentials in clean energy.

In terms of solar radiation, the mean range is 3.5KWh/M2-day in the south and 7.0KWh/M2-day in the north since 2014 (NREEP, 2014). Nebo (2015) informs that, through government support to the

Energy Commission of Nigeria (ECN), over 700 off grid solar home systems were installed in 12 rural communities. This he says is aimed at supporting national efforts to provide alternative energy sources to rural communities, especially those not on the national grid. In addition, a total of 10 solar photovoltaic (PV) water borehole systems were installed in these communities. These are now enabling community members to have access to cleaner sources of water.

Nebo also observes concern by government that the absence of energy accounts for rural deforestation as a source for cooking and heating. This led to the supply of locally sourced clay stoves for some communities. There are also improvements in the provision of basic amenities like pipe borne water and better healthcare supported by solar power in some places.

Referring to government activities directly related to climate change, Nigeria's Minister of Environment in 2009, John Odey, hinted of Nigeria's desire to mitigate climate change (Koblowsky & Speranza, 2010). He listed a set of mitigation projects initiated by his ministry and the Special Climate Change Unit (SCCU), including predominantly clean development projects. Notable here are two projects to forestall gas flaring – a methane accumulation facility for waste management and afforestation projects. Dr. Victor Fodeke, Chair Special Climate Change Fund, estimated that consistent implementation of Nigerian CDM projects could attract investments worth over US$ 600 million (Koblowsky & Speranza, 2010).

From the foregoing, Nigeria has made efforts to realize her UNFCCC commitments, in spite of her limited capacity. The country has also participated in high level meetings of the UNFCCC. At the 2016 COP 22 Session held in Marrakech the country was well represented with about 40 delegates, comprising representatives of the National Assembly, State Governors, Federal Ministries, Departments and Agencies (MDAS), State Governments, Non-Governmental Organizations (NGOs), academia and the Media (Isabel & Agbarakwe, 2016).

PROPOSALS TO IMPROVE NIGERIA'S COMPLIANCE WITH THE UNFCCC

Regarding solutions to improve Nigeria's compliance measures in line with the UNFCCC as stated in question 1, political will, financial and technical support from developed countries, inclusion of renewable energy in school curriculum as well as more engagement by media, NGOs and rural dwellers, were among many other measures for Nigeria's climate action. Hitherto, the FNC, SNC and NDC provide elaborate details on the way forward for Nigeria's climate action.

The FNC proposes the following under physical and ecological adaptation:

  i. Encouragement of the promotion of diverse projects on biodiversity;
  ii. Reduced population;
  iii. Establishment of protected areas;
  iv. Implantation of agricultural systems that protect from soil erosion;
  v. Establishment of mechanical and engineering structures to deck erosion;
  vi. Relocation of affection people;
  vii. Adoption of new livelihoods and living conditions;
  viii. Minimize biomass burning and woodland destruction;
  ix. Development of resistant plant species to temperature and rainfall;
  x. Change cultivation method with minimum tillage;
  xi. Creation of conditions for profitable agricultural activities ;
  xii. Meteorological agencies to alert farmers on weather forecasts;
  xiii. Reduction in livestock density and alteration of animal distribution;
  xiv. Discourage the use of marginal lands and protecting areas that are degraded;
  xv. Public awareness and veterinary extension services;
  xvi. Promotion water recycling and re-use;
  xvii. Development of monitoring of ground water supplies ;
  xviii. Improve rain harvesting technologies and back up tanks.

The FNC further proposes the following under socio-economic cultural sectors:

i. Increase awareness;
ii. Diversification of the economy;
iii. Relocation of threatened transmission facilities;
iv. Develop and enhance renewable resources like solar energy;
v. Relocation of industries to favourable sites;
vi. Careful design of transport systems taking into account expected impact of climate change on the structure of facilities;
vii. Consistent purging of vector population;
viii. Strengthen health system;
ix. Improved sanitation and immunization;
x. Use both hard and soft protections to secure coastal areas e.g. dykes, seawalls, beach nourishment and afforestation;
xi. Change in planting dates and cultivars;
xii. Development of alternative habitat areas.

The SNC proposes the following mitigation measures some of which are already in operation:

i. Through clean development mechanism, ample opportunities are provided for conversion of unflared gas to cooking gas. Two projects in Kwale delta state namely Kwale Oil Gas processing plant and Kwale Gas utilization project account for 1,496,934 tCO2 and 2,626,735 tCO2 respectively. There's also a third project on efficient wood stove with potential for 31,309, tCO2 emission reduction.
ii. Apply invasive species for bio-fuels;
iii. Expand use of solar energy for residences, institutions, cooking and agriculture;
iv. Expansion of public transport system;
v. Expand forestry programmes to satisfy wood demand and vegetation cover through afforestation, agro-forestry and forest protection;
vi. Suitable tillage practice such as fallow and crop rotation;
vii. Improved water management for irrigation;
viii. Application of organic fertilizer;
ix. Improving animal production through efficient veterinary care;
x. Emphasis on small stocks with lower emissions like fish and snails.
xi. Sensitization on bush burning;

xii. Securing funds from foreign partners to cover climate change costs and improvements.

In terms of adaptation, the SNC recommends these adaptive strategies:

i. Further studies on water resources management and development;
ii. Efficient irrigation system e.g. drip irrigation;
iii. Use of biodegradable suppressants to curtail evaporation(40% reduction);
iv. Explore more water harvesting options for agriculture and domestic use;
v. Protection of water bodies from pollution;
vi. Strengthening the FADAMA project in view of its success on cooperation farming;
vii. Adopting drought tolerant seed varieties;
viii. Development of diverse capacities for livelihood;
ix. Improvement of forecasting in a timely manner;
x. Cultivating cover crops for soil protection;
xi. Stabilization of gullies and erosion sites;
xii. Raising transport routes to make them passable;
xiii. Building business to push back ocean surges;
xiv. Relocation of vulnerable communities;
xv. Revegetation of degraded areas to promote biodiversity and stop desertification;
xvi. Oil companies to scale up oil spill monitoring technologies with remote sensing and Geological Information System;
xvii. Create Awareness among host communities of pipeline routes to stop damages;
xviii. Encouragement of private sector to participate in electricity generation and contribute to the national grid;
xix. Efficient stoves to reduce consumption of fuel wood;
xx. Architectural designs suitable for climate change;
xxi. Engage private sector in climate change issues;
xxii. Erecting green belts around cities;
xxiii. Develop inventory of local materials that can strengthen industrial transit to renewal methods of production.

In the NDC, under mitigation, it proffers decentralised renewable energy under the energy subsector with multi-cycle power stations, scalable power stations of 20-50 megawatts as well as enforced energy efficient use of natural gas rather than liquid fuels. The oil and gas subsector require improved enforcement of gas flaring restrictions bearing in mind the scenario in figure 9.1. Here we refer to development of gas to power plant as gas flare suites(micro-grid), blending 10% by volume of fuel ethanol with gasoline(E10) and 20% by volume of biodiesel with petroleum diesel(B20) for transportation fuels. Agricultural and land use sector require climate smart agriculture, cessation of charcoal use. Industrial sub sector requires benchmarking against international best practice for industrial energy use, adoption of green technology in industry. The transport subsector requires modal shift from air to high speed rail, moving freight to rail, upgrading roads, urban transit, toll roads/road pricing, increase use of compressed natural gas, reform petrol/diesel subsidies (NDC, 2016, p.11). In proffering the above, the document warns that these could only be achieved through diligent application of the strategic framework for voluntary nationally appropriate mitigation action. At the time of publishing the report, NAMA was yet to be developed. With the country's complaint of scarce fund and technical capacity, this mitigation challenge will subsist without external financial support. And with the perennial practice of policy and strategy changes by succeeding governments, attending to the problems of the NDC's over mitigation is pertinent. Overcoming this hurdle requires addressing a number of policy issues. Chapters nine and ten flag key concerns that must be addressed for significant climate action to manifest and be generally appreciated.

Table 8.5: Summary of Renewal Energy Capital Projects By Government From 2005-2017

Year	Wind		Solar PV		Solar PV Mini-Grid		Solar PV Water Pumping		Re-Total Mega	Transformers	
	Qty	Mega Watt	Qty	Mega Watt	Qty	Mega Watt	Qty	Mega Watt	Watt	Qty	Capacity
2005	-	-	-	-	1	0.005	1	0.0011	000.61	-	-
2006	-	-	-	-	4	0.02	2	0.0005	0.0205	-	-
2007	3	0.0075	-	-	1	0.005	-	-	0.0125	-	-
2008	3	0.03	1200	0.096	-	-	5	0.006	0.132	-	-
2009	3	0.03	18541	2.318	-		98	0.117	2.465	-	-
2010	-	-	25611	4.098	5	0.068	296	0.375	4.541	-	-
2011	4	0.002	5100	0.816	1	0.04	72	0.086	0.944	-	-
2012	-	-	7000	1.1	9	0.061	246	0.295	1.456	-	-
2013	-	-	7522	1.204	4	0.016	88	0.106	1.326	-	-
2014	-	-	3010	0.566	2	0.018	39	0.0468	0.6308	-	-
2015	-	-	2959	0.5918	2	0.02	41	0.0492	0.661	-	-
2016	-	-	1815	0.363	10	0.042	85	0.102	0.507	-	-
2017	-	-	1100	0.22	13	0.51	36	0.043	0.314	10	500/33 KVA
Total									13.0159		500/33 KVA

Source: Energy Commission of Nigeria (2018)

Table 8.6: CDM Project with CERs as at October 2009

Name of CDM Project Activity	Type of Project	UN Reg. Date	Annual Emission Reduction (tCO2/y)
Recovery of associated gas project that would otherwise be flared at Kwale oil gas processing plant	Waste gas/heat utilization	Nov 9th, 2006	1,496,934
Gas utilization project	Waste gas/heat utilization	Feb 10th 2009	2,626,735
Efficient Fuel Wood Stoves for	Energy efficiency	Oct 12th,	31,309

Source: SNC (2014)

Table 8.7: Proposed CDM Projects

Name of CDM Project Activity	Type of Project	Annual Emission Reduction Potentials (tCO2/y)
Improved cooking stoves for Nigeria programme of activities (PoA)	Energy efficiency	8,912
Distribution of fuel-efficient improved cooking stoves in Nigeria (PoA)	Energy efficiency	46,717
African improved cooking stoves (PoA)	Energy efficiency	15,477
Municipal Solid Waste Composting Project in Ikorodu, Lagos State	Methane recovery & utilization	281,781
Landfill gas (LFG project in Nigeria)	Methane recovery utilization	129,932
Multi country small scale CDM program of activity for reduction of emission from non-renewable fuel from cooking at household level	Renewable energy	51,385
Lafarge WAPCO partial substitution of alternative fuels in cement facilities project in Nigeria	Cement	166,557
Recovery & Marketing of Gas that would otherwise be flared at the Asuokpa/ Umutu Marginal Field, Nigeria	Waste gas/heat utilization	256,793

Source: SNC (2014)

CHAPTER NINE

TRIAD PLOT FOR DOMESTIC STAKEHOLDERS' ACTION

I. REPOSITIONING STAKEHOLDERS IN DOMESTIC CLIMATE ACTION

In chapter eight, we analysed the outcome of a previous field survey of active stakeholders influencing climate governance in Nigeria vis-à-vis documented evidence from industry. Our conclusion was that NGOs drive climate action as influencers followed by the public sector, with a few clean and renewable projects, while the corporate private sector operates from the rear. This general perception raises concern for the private sector as a critical stakeholder.

It is incontestable that if Nigeria's climate action must yield positive results there must be repositioning. The private sector must drive innovation in clean technology. As exemplars, initiatives by the private sector are evident in the clean energy partnerships in the markets in Kano and Aba that run on off-grid solar power. The Pan African University Lagos also has a domiciled climate Innovation Centre. It is instructive to underscore that these private sector actions are executed with the initiative and support of the NGOs, knowing that progress can only be made only if the private sector is fully involved in climate actions (Koblowsky & Speranza, 2010). Hence, greater investment in green and clean technology deserve more participation by the private sector in Nigeria. The most visible activities of the private sector in climate action are based on individual efforts in the purchase of solar panels that are not corporate in nature nor coordinated for planning purposes. As a result, records are unavailable to support a lot of Nigeria's drive in climate action. Agricultural practices are not left out in this technological pursuit. The sovereign green bond initiated by the federal public sector is also a veritable medium to be harnessed by the private sector to increase climate action (Koblowsky & Speranza, 2010).

As for the public sector, the establishment of Agencies focusing on environment and climate change is a testament to its frontline position in climate action. In fact, the proliferation of these agencies has resulted in more awareness of the environmental challenges of climate change by the general public and policy makers. The public sector also acts through policy formulation on climate change and participation at meetings on climate change. Normally, when it comes to climate governance, the public sector should be the epicentre of coordination. But progress on the part of public sector is hampered by inadequate funding, poor capacity and poor economic base resulting in her relegation by the NGOs (Koblowsky & Speranza, 2010). There is also the issue of political will. It has been argued that Nigeria's oil-dependent economy as a developing country, affects the political will to address the problem. This is a major drawback for the public sector that is usually driven by the political class.

Given the limitation of public sectors in developing countries to initiate climate action as recognized by the UNFCCC, it is no surprise that NGOs have led climate action advocacy efforts in Nigeria. As we have observed earlier, even in the 1980s and 1990s, it is agency-action through NGOs that raised public awareness on the need to focus on the environment. The writings of Kenule Saro Wiwa which concentrated on environmental activism, rallied public support on the destruction of the environment by the oil majors in the Niger Delta. The actions of NGOs resulted in the creation of Federal Environmental Protection Agencies and Ministries of Environment at the federal and state levels. Since the adoption of the millenium and sustainable development goals at the turn of the century, leading environmental activist like Nnimmo Bassey, Priscilla Achakpa, Desmond Majekodunmi joined by younger advocates like Gloria Bulus and her generation have sustained the momentum in climate change advocacy.

There are also significant initiatives by NGOs outside Nigeria. In 2013, Friends of the Earth, leading a coalition of NGOs instituted court action in Netherlands on behalf of oil producing communities in the Niger Delta (Oluduro, 2015). The action resulted in a favourable judgment amounting to millions of dollars to the communities. NGOs were similarly responsible for a court action in London against shell for its failure to install spill detection and warning devices on its pipelines (Oluduro, 2015). In the final analysis, NGOs have more experience in environmental action in Nigeria and so have developed better capacity over the years.

II. WHOLISTIC ENGAGEMENT OF THE MEDIA IN DOMESTIC CLIMATE ACTION

It is however unfortunate that despite efforts to coordinate the activities of climate change NGOs to work strategically, these organisations still prefer to be autonomous. The present scenario where NGOs work independent of each other creates disharmony in the strategy for climate action in Nigeria (Koblowsky & Speranza, 2010). The NGOs are currently the main sources of capacity building on climate action in the country. Without harmonizing their activities in this regard, there is great tendency for duplication of capacities in one area while skills are lacking in critical specialisations. At the moment, it is the NGOs that train more journalists and sponsor more reports and awareness campaign in the media. The British Broadcasting Corporation (BBC) in a 2008 report established that public perception of climate change is impacted by the media (Batta, Ashong & Bashir, 2013). The report found that the media and schools constitute Nigerians' main source of information. Unfortunately, the NGOs' support to the media have not been sufficient to build climate change awareness to the desired level. The result is that, the grasp of the issues in climate change by the Nigerian media is poor. This is akin to the scenario in other developing countries. Mare (2011) reflects the same situation in South Africa where he says media reports are fond of making sweeping comments to create impact without reflecting urgency of the situation or contextualizing it to facilitate understanding.

In the case of Nigeria, climate change issues are hardly reported except there is a major event or even, when controversial issues arising from climate change occur (Ukonu, Akpan & Anorue, 2012). Otherwise if it is not newsworthy, climate issues are rarely reported and without follow-up. The focus is usually on current news and timely events that result in print-sales and viewership. And this general inclination of remaining with news stories makes climate change not to receive the in-depth analysis it deserves. Another time when climate change issues are reported is in the appeal for fund or assistance. One analyst puts it succinctly when he said that throughout the tenure of Nigeria's former minister of environment John Odey's appearance in the media "out of nine times…it was only in one story that he did not talk about funds or aid to Nigeria to tackle climate change (Ukonu, Akpan & Anorue 2012, p.28). Interestingly, there were no follow-up stories on this appeal for aid. Take for instance a vanguard story of Tuesday 15 December 2009 containing a news item of the US pledge of millions of LED batteries to the developing world facing electricity challenges. There was no follow up to the story (Ukonu, Akpan & Anorue 2012).

It is unfortunate that climate change coverage by the media is low with specific focus on agreements, funds and meetings. The issue of biophysical occurrences are seldom reported. This imbalance in media coverage in Nigeria results in shallow reports. Giving readers and the public shallow understanding of the complexity of the issues. Meanwhile, it is a statement of fact that, the manner of media coverage of scientific subjects affects public perception which also influences policy.

Consequently, with low reportage of the activities of NGOs, public sector and private sector on climate action in Nigeria, very few persons in position of leadership in the country are informed about climate change. This is what happens when the media coverage is inadequate and cannot be said to be purposefully pursued to achieve societal change. It is in this light that Nwabueze (2007) observes that the press in Nigeria is failing even in covering pollution in the Niger Delta that is localized, not to talk of gas flaring or oil exploration which is 30% of carbon emission nationwide (Batta, Ashong & Bashir, 2012). This brings to fore the concern of a former Group Managing Director of the Nigerian National Petroleum

Corporation (NNPC) Dr. Mohammed Barkindo that poor media showing on environment is connected to the fact that the issue is not vital in the national corporate agenda (Batta, Ashong & Bashir).

The onus is therefore on the media in Nigeria to step up to this challenge in the area of climate change. In effect, the Nigerian journalist has not mastered the complexity of climate change. Given this state of affairs, "Nigerian newspapers can scale up their coverage as well as engaging in framing of climate change issues in terms of what communities can do (Batta, Ashong & Bashir, 2012, p.61). These may include greening of neighbourhoods, landscaping, and reflective roofing sheets. Through framing, the wordings of a situation are constructed to affect mental perception. It is to influence thinking by involving interpretative schemes (Schenfele, 2000, p.309). Using framing, a journalist decides what to emphasise to promote action on them. From the study conducted by Batta, Ashong & Bashir (2012) we see that the few stories on climate change emphasised mitigation. It occupied 58.2% of the coding frame. Terms like alternative energy, carbon reduction, emission reduction, and green technology are common in the literature. There is also huge emphasis on the catastrophe and the urgency for action. Meanwhile mitigation is only obligatory for developed countries which Nigeria is not a part of. So, in most cases the actions that are promoted by these stories cannot be acted upon by communities or public sector's concerned.

The Nigerian newspapers lose the narrative by advocating pro-emission solution to climate change governance in the country. There is the overriding tendency to overlook the provision of the UNFCCC which enjoins developing countries to pursue adaptation by taking measures that will build resilience to climate change. For the ordinary person to be involved, the narrative should be framed to focus on natural climate occurrence that he can associate with and solutions on how to survive them. Otherwise, the current mitigation framing excludes a lot of people who cannot afford to mitigate. Talking about mix farming, new skills and tree planting as adaptation methods elicit better result. But as concurred by the interviewees, the media are like appendages to the NGOs and so will reflect and frame their reports to suit their sponsors. And so many in the media only reflect the message of its sponsors. In the case of Nigeria, the NGOs are mostly euro-centric climate change advocates with emphasis on mitigation. Principally, countries like Germany, France and Britain and a few others which the country owes gratitude for the little assistance in mitigation climate action. It is therefore natural that the emphasis in the media is on complex mitigation action that in most cases are cumbersome and distant to associate with the remote reality of the local communities. So in fairness to many many outfits, they are transmitting the agenda of their sponsors, which are the euro-centric climate change advocates.

With the above in view, a fundamental approach to change the narrative from mitigation to adaptation will be to approach NGOs from countries that promote a different agenda. These will include the United States of America, Canada and the Russian Federation among others. Given the critical role of NGOs in Nigeria's climate action, there is the need to invite more social forces from these countries to involve in climate action. Developed countries from both divides are enjoined by the UNFCCC to assist developing countries. At the moment, the engagement of these external social forces is low and adding to slow progress in the country's climate action.

III. BUILDING DOMESTIC CAPACITY IN CLIMATE ACTION

The UNFCCC in her review of national capacities also identified significant gaps in the participation of key stakeholders in climate action globally. In 2004 for instance, it was established that the lack of participation by key stakeholders in national polices on capacity building was a great setback (Zinnkan, 2014). A review by the UNFCCC of capacity building policy in 2007 called for capacity building to be included in national development strategies. Another review by the same body in 2016 identified the lack of clear process to enhance the effectiveness of capacity building as the major challenge. This review frowned at capacity building being undertaken on ad-hoc basis as practiced over the years in most developing countries where Nigeria belongs. The few exceptions among the developing countries have been encouraged to serve as role models. Using Kenya, Rwanda and Ethiopia as examples, the African Development Bank is at the forefront of developing the capacities of the public and private sectors to harness investment opportunities in climate change and other green growth initiatives (AfDB, 2014). The bank is able to do so in these countries owing to coordination in their climate action. In these exemplary countries, because climate change is impacting business, new knowledge and opportunities in climate change are being developed through capacity building (Zinnkann, 2014). These lessons are reference points for Nigeria to emulate as encouraged in Art. 4 of the UNFCCC which calls on climate change to be included in socio-economic planning and policy implementation.

CHAPTER TEN

THE FUTURE OF CLIMATE ACTION IN NIGERIA

FUNDAMENTAL ELEMENTS FOR CLIMATE ACTION IN NIGERIA UNDER THE UNFCCC

In view of the UNFCCC's conditional compliance for developing countries, Nigeria's future compliance in response to developed countries will require a re-examining of intervention in three critical areas: Finance, Capacity Building and Technology transfer. These constitute the fundamental elements for climate action in any developing country.

FINANCING CLIMATE ACTION

Of the many challenges militating against Nigeria's implementation of her climate change commitments, her low economy is principally the overriding factor (Adache, 2013). Both mitigation and adaptation are capital intensive which is a huge burden for many developing countries including Nigeria. Even the cost of adaptation identified as the area of priority for developing countries is still highly prohibitive to be left on their own to bear. Unfortunately, as disclosed by one of Nigeria's foremost climate change governance expert, Professor Chukwumerije Okereke, the country has performed poorly in attracting international climate finance (Thisday Newspaper, 2018). As a developing country and regional power, this performance is an indication of the country's less than impressive approach toward climate action. Even on the African continent, Rwanda, Kenya, South Africa and Ethiopia have performed better than Nigeria. Kenya for instance generates 60% of its energy need from renewable energy through international assistance (Gichira, Agwata & Muigua, 2014). This is something that is doable in Nigeria if there can be a shift from oil money to seek available blue and green opportunities in other sectors. For instance, some emission reduction projects in Nigeria could be repackaged to attract climate finance. According to Professor Chukwumerije, the Abuja, Lagos and Port Harcourt light rail projects have huge potentials to displace many vehicles on the road, thereby reducing tonnes of carbondioxide emissions. These could have been presented to attract funding from the Green Climate Fund (GCF).

But owing to the lack of coherent green growth plan and strategy, Nigeria is unable to attract such global climate finance. Even the climate change bill in the National Assembly, which is intended to legislate climate change into the country's laws as obtainable in other developing countries, is yet to pass into law more than ten years after its introduction to the national assembly. And this is supposed to be a preparatory step to serious action on climate change. According to Okereke (Vanguard Newspaper, 2018), this poor preparation could cost Nigeria 30% of her GDP by 2050. This is between 100 billion dollars to 460 billion dollars. In the words of Nigeria's former Minister of Finance and current Director General of the World Trade Organisation, Dr. Ngozi Okonjo Iweala in a report by the Global Commission on the Economy and Climate Change, released in June 2018 at the UN Headquarters in New York, climate change opens a global opportunity of 26 trillion dollars in low carbon economy (Global Commission Report, 2018). This report invites action in five economic sectors: industry, energy, food, land use as well as energy. Specifically she says, climate change can generate 65 new low carbon jobs and avoid 700 premature deaths from pollution. The UN Secretary General, Anthony Guterres in the same report re-echoed Iweala's thoughts in saying that even fossil fuel dependent countries are diversifying with over 250 investors with 28 trillion dollars in managed assets signing onto a climate economy initiative called Climate Action 100+ (Global Commission Report, 2018). Considering these costs and benefits, it is imperative on Nigeria to strengthen her designated authorities/institutions by improving their ability to plan and design bankable project on renewal energy, smart agriculture, and sustainable land management and flood control measures that can attract funding from GCF and other sources of climate finance, which are readily available. The current nature of the projects executed by public sectors as indicated in table 9.5 from the Energy Commission of Nigeria will hardly attract the private sector into the clean energy industry. From the table, the total energy generated from renewal sources from 2005-2017 barely amounts to 13 megawatts. This can hardly impact the country's economy that is based on 500 billion dollars at the time. Yet opportunities for renewable energy investment abound. A good example is the AFAM Power station with potential to produce 926 megawatts while significantly reducing emission.

The other option will be to bring in external finance from developed countries. The UNFCCC affirms that developed "states shall provide financial resources to assist developing country parties" (UNFCCC Art. 4). Article 11 of the convention makes provision for the operation of a financial mechanism under one or more international entities. In this regard, private entities as well as public institutions are encouraged to make resources available in the area of mitigation and adaption. Developing countries may avail themselves of the following financial mechanisms: UN REDD Program, Special Climate Change Fund (SCCF), Least Developed Countries Fund (LDCF), the Climate Investment Fund (CIF), Green Climate Fund (GCF), Adaptation Fund (AF) and Global Environmental Facility (GEF). The UNFCCC sees these funds as legitimate compensation to developing countries for the damages by developed countries resulting to climate change(Sharna, 2016). Other sources of finance that could be harnessed by Nigeria outside the UNFCCC include Pilot-Programme for Climate Resilience (PPCR), Clean Technology Fund (CTF), Forest Carbon Partnership Facility (FCPF), International Climate Initiative (ICI), Forest Investment Program(FIP) and the Global Climate Change Alliance (GCCA) among the key sponsors.

CAPACITY BUILDING FOR CLIMATE ACTION

There is also concern on capacity building under the UNFCCC which is synonymous with institution building, institutional strengthening, human resources development and institutional economics (Sharna, 2016). Article 6 of the convention announces its dedication to promote education, public awareness, public participation and training of personnel in addressing climate change. The convention enjoins all parties to engage and cooperate in research on the global climate system. Hence, the National Communications of countries are expected to contain information on these. Here, assistance to developing countries to build capacity to address global warming is considered a responsibility for the developed countries (UNFCCC 2003). Thus, in view of the vulnerable status and constraint of developing countries in climate action, capacity building should be the first step to the solution. And overcoming any constraint to capacity building is crucial to Nigeria's effective compliance and implementation of her commitments most especially with respect to climate adaptation under the UNFCCC.

Looking at the grave impact of climate change both ecologically and socio-economically as depicted in Nigeria's National Communications, it is clear that the capacity to first of all adapt to climate change is a critical need. These areas of acute need include preparing national communications, preparing drawings on financial mechanisms, technology transfer etc. Even her ability to take climate action to fulfil her Nationally Determined Contribution is dependent on effective capacity building frameworks or institutions. Institution here refers to active agencies that are dedicated to climate change adaptation or mitigation like the climate change bill awaiting final passage in the National Assembly. This will be a far cry from the current ad-hoc arrangement of public sector departments merely designating desk officers for climate change. As we have seen from the survey feedback, without institutional backing or political will, these desks are insignificant to a comprehensive roadmap on climate change in Nigeria. The clamour therefore is for institutions that will harmonise the various environmental policies in order to come up with one effective legal authority on climate action in Nigeria. Related environmental policies like the national policy on drought and desertification, national policy on erosion, flood control and coastal zone management, national forest policy, national biodiversity strategy and action plan could be adapted and harmonized to one institution to build adaptation response efforts (Oladipo, 2010, p, 20). The delay or failure in building this institution indicates Nigeria's limited capacity while in dire need for it. Without capacity building, even where these institutions are created, the probability of their success is highly unlikely as witnessed in other areas (Ayoade, 2004).

Fortunately, the UNFCCC at COP 21 makes provision for assistance through its Capacity Building Initiative for Transparency (CBIT), most especially in developing countries of which Nigeria is one. Through the Global Environmental Fund, projects from developing countries could be prioritised for action. In fact, over 13 thematic and financial entities involved in capacity building under the UNFCCC are available for Nigeria to explore (Sharna, 2017, p. 16). Under the thematic entities, there are Adaptation Committee, Climate Technology Centre And Network (CTCN), Consultative Group of Experts on National Communication from Non-Annex I Parties, Warsaw International Mechanism for Loss and Damages, Executive Board Of Clean Development Mechanisms, Least Developed Countries Expert Group, Standing Committee on Finance and the Technology Executive Committee. The financial entities include the operating entities of the convention's financial mechanism (GEF, LDC Fund, Special Climate Change Fund, Adaptation Fund, and the Green Climate Fund or GCF) (Sharna, 2017, p.16).

Banking on the above support under the UNFCCC, Nigeria would increase her capacity in human resources, greater network between actors as well as institutional capacity which are clearly stipulated in the NDC (2016). These are central to the immediate concerns for adaptation. The areas of mitigation which is a subsidiary and conditional commitment for developing countries under the UNFCCC can also be negotiated with the availability of resources.

As underscored above, the convention recognizes that capacity is the overriding edge that developed countries have over developing countries (UNFCCC Art. 4.2) and therefore makes extra provisions to encourage capacity building in developing countries in several respect. For instance, Article 10 of the Kyoto Protocol for annex I countries provides for strengthening research capacity and institutional strengthening in developing countries. In 2001, the COP 7 in Marrakech provides a guiding principle for capacity building in developing countries that is country-driven and builds on existing structures and should be integrated. Further decisions on capacity building were taken at the Conference of Parties summit in Delhi – 2007, Durban-2011, Doha-2012, 2014 and Paris-2015. Given these enabling international frameworks, there is definitely ample opportunity for more capacity development in Nigeria.

TECHNOLOGY TRANSFER AND CLIMATE ACTION

The issue of clean technology is central to every countries' climate action. For a country relying on fossil fuel for most of its energy need, this transition could be delicate. But the responses from our survey indicate that climate change poses a complex menace to livelihood and the environment. This should be of concern to any government. Thus, in the global effort to contain and overcome the climate change threat, technology has been identified as the most appropriate response to address the challenges posed by climate change. Unfortunately, there's a global gap in technology-based mitigation and adaptation capabilities (Olawuyi, 2017). Simply put "the low carbon and climate resilient technologies that are required for climate change mitigation and adaptation are simply not available" (Olawuyi, 2017, p.2). The situation is worse in developing countries like Nigeria. Yet technology is the most realistic means by which developing countries can expedite action on climate change. Article 4(5) of the UNFCCC provides that developed countries "shall promote, facilitate and finance as appropriate, the transfer of or access to environmentally sound technologies and know-how". The call to developed countries here is to provide developing countries with the needed capabilities to reduce emissions.

Technology transfer and absorption are indeed critical to Nigeria's compliance or implementation of any agreements under the UNFCCC. This encompasses the ability "to receive, adopt and learn from the acquired technology so that it can develop its own domestic capacity (UNECA, 2010, p. 56). Under the UNFCC, there's already the Clean Development Mechanism, but the lukewarm flow of these technology cannot ensure adequate climate action. Given the surplus of renewable energy sources in Nigeria, one would expect that industries, households and agriculture would be predominantly run by these sources of energy. Nigeria's Vice President Yemi Osinbajo underscores the centrality of technology in Nigeria's climate change response when he declares that "the creation of an enabling environment for climate smart business to thrive is simply the only way to go" (Vanguard, 2018). The call here is for the deployment of climate technology solutions in agriculture, industry, transport and other development subsectors.

Solar, wind, water and natural gas have been identified as veritable media for clean energy application in Nigeria. Off grid solar energy is the most available and most impactful green technology in Nigeria with uses in homes and industries which could be improved upon. Public sector on her part should try to encourage investments and initiatives in the private solar sector through its Solar Home Project and Energizing Economy initiatives that provide electricity to residences and commercial areas (Vanguard, 2018). Already, from public sector collaboration with the NGOs and private sector, 13,000 shops in Sabon-Gari market in Kano-Nigeria enjoy off grid solar power solution. Ariaria market in Abia state, Sura market in Lagos state, as well as markets in Edo, Oyo and Ondo States in Nigeria are in line for these stand-alone solar systems. What is self-evident from these is that technology is "a powerful solution for simultaneously addressing climate change and advancing development" (Tarfa, 2017, p.10). With a weak economy driven by 500 billion dollars for a population of about 200 million persons, Nigeria would definitely need the intervention of developed countries to transit to clean technology.

In addition, the existence of clean development mechanism under the UNFCCC provides ample opportunity for Nigeria to leverage upon, bearing in mind that since the commencement of Clean Development Mechanism (CDM) projects in Africa, the technology in-flow soared above 800 percent (Olawuyi, 2017). This was even before 2008. With a Presidential implementation committee on CDM, what is left for Nigeria are visible concrete actions to reflect the seriousness with which Nigeria approaches the issue of clean technology.

But again, technology acquisition does not occur in a vacuum. The receiving country must create the enabling environment for these technologies to thrive when received. In Nigeria a number of barriers need to be overcome for technology transfer to be effective. Olawuyi (2017) lists domestic barriers to be overcome before addressing these climate technology gaps, namely cultural and traditional barriers, weak legal protection for imported technologies, lack of capacity, and weak investment-environment for clean technology entrepreneurship. A brief expose on these barriers by Olawuyi would provide clarity.

i. Cultural barrier: cultural resistance to foreign technology is a major concern. In this context he says foreign technologies are rejected for cultural or political reasons. A case in point is the Kwale CDM project designed to capture diverted flared gas at the oil-gas processing plant. This was resisted because of local concerns on the implications on "traditional lands and forests." Of course one cannot but agree that public sector's failure to engage the local communities is responsible for some of these prejudices, but this concern remains a bottleneck, as it arises from mistrust between public sectors and indigenous communities.

ii. Weak legal protection for imported technologies: this relates to inventors' concern that their innovations will not be deployed or adapted without their authorization. In Nigeria, this is reflected in the exclusion of some technologies from patentability (Olawuyi, 2017, p.3). The Nigerian patent and design act for instance allows public sector to arbitrarily exclude some innovations from patentability and is ambiguous on the inclusion of climate change technologies in this category.

iii. Related to the above is public sector's granting of already patented licences of products to third parties without the consent of the innovators or compensation for their innovation. The Nigerian law does not codify the safeguards which are contained in international conventions on intellectual property to protect the innovators. Rather the Nigeria law provides that once a license is granted, the license owner is not bound to pay any form of fee to the patentee. In a country in need of innovation to protect its people and economy from climate change, these weak legislations that enable public sector to leverage on intellectual property should be strengthened and revitalized to instil confidence and improve the flow of technology for climate actions.

iv. Lack of Capacity: Poor technological capability is a major constraint. Here the absence of a critical mass of technically skilled university graduates is part of the reason the use of imported technology is not consistent. According to the African Development bank, only 25% enroll for courses in science and mathematics in universities. Meanwhile the assimilation of technology requires a large pool of such skilled experts in the utilization of clean technology options. This therefore calls for public sectors to identify training needs in climate science in order to provide adequate knowledge on them.

v. Weak investment-environment for clean technology entrepreneurship: Nigeria's weak economic, social and environmental conditions constitute a challenge to entrepreneurial activity to develop commercial climate technology. This further weakens her ability to continually attract clean technology companies that want to market their products at an early stage of development. Olawuyi says what is required therefore is for national public sectors to provide the right incentives for clean technology (cleantech) entrepreneurs to spearhead homegrown technological solutions. Using the sovereign green bond, the public sector could provide capital to cleantech firms to grow their business in Nigeria. This is the example of fast developing countries like "China, India and Malaysia that have committed significant clean technology and have over the years been rewarded with geometric rise of start-up cleantech companies and increased technology (Olawuyi, 2017, p.5). With such incentives, China witnessed 10% rise in cleantech investment in 2016. Sadly in Nigeria, the country is witnessing disincentives for clean energy entrepreneurs. For instance, only in 2017, the public sector imposed additional 10% duty on all solar panels imported into the country

(Henry Boll, 2018). This is quite unfortunate bearing in mind the nascent nature of the sector with no solar energy manufacturing plant in the country. Such policy actions for whatever reason, sabotage the country's drive towards sustainable clean energy that is affordable.

The elements streamlined above for Nigeria are also in accordance with the convention, the protocol and the Paris agreement. It is expected that they will also be country-specific to facilitate concrete climate actions. The conclusion here is that, their adoption will be crucial to Nigeria's implementation of her benchmarks and compliance with the UNFCCC.

CHAPTER ELEVEN

WRAP-UP: SURVIVING GLOBAL DISTRUST IN CLIMATE ACTION

RESETTING THE FAILING GLOBAL ACTION AND NIGERIA'S CLIMATE GOVERNANCE PHILOSOPHY

The global governance of climate change offers an interesting perspective on the difficulty to enforce compliance in terms of mitigation and adaptation for developing countries. As we have seen in the past, the United States pulled out of the Paris agreement, Canada pulled out of the Kyoto Protocol while China remains the biggest global polluter. These are countries that are major stakeholders in any global agreement on climate change. Among other things, their volte-faces have become compliance irritants in the eyes of developing countries under the UNFCCC. David Ciplet provides a poignant implication of what it portends for developing countries who must walk the delicate line between developed countries that support mitigation and those that oppose the initiatives. For him, this dilemma for developing countries necessitates the need for their scholars to situate their domestic initiatives against prevailing global initiatives. But the problem with realising this is that, based on the UNFCCC, developing countries should depend on developed countries in their compliance initiatives. Amidst this global dilemma, what is the way forward for developing countries?

As we have seen in Nigeria's climate action for instance, the country's implementation action and compliance initiatives as reflected in her communication with the UNFCCC demonstrates her dependence on developed countries to fulfill her mandate. Such behaviour where climate action is reliant on assistance from external sources exposes the power-dynamics at play in compliance action under the UNFCCC. This is similar to what Robert Cox terms "a neo-Gramscian framework of negotiated consent" (Ciplet, 2015, p.248). In Ciplet's explanation, developing countries' ability to participate, comprehend or change social structures is constrained by the same structures. The reason for this he says is because these states are already institutionalized into an existing order where the international regime is shaped by micro processes of bottom-up bargaining and constrained by existing macro structures of production relations and ideational formations (Ciplet, 2015, p.255). In fact under the UNFCCC, the special recognition accorded to the developed countries in the responsibility for mitigation and adaptation presupposes that the interest of the developed countries is already a given. It is the interests of the developing countries that seek to be factored in the scheme of things. After all, "power presupposes that account be taken of the interests and tendencies of the groups over which power is to be exercise (Ciplet, 2015, p. 256).

What this means is that, a developing country participating in climate change agreements is already determined by the power dynamics of the agreement. Hence, the behaviours of Nigeria under the UNFCCC is determined by an international regime that is power based. Drawing from this structural conditioning, the ability of a country like Nigeria to influence international policy is greatly limited. In this vein, the chances of Nigeria's domestic social forces which comprise both state and non-state actors to engender compliance against the will of decision makers in the developed world is highly improbable. These limitations include "historically specific limits to organizing capability, disadvantageous positioning in global economy, world views, ecological conditions, production relations, dependence on specific capital interests and disproportionate vulnerability to forms of coercion such as bribes, divisive strategies and threats (Ciplet, 2015, p. 257). If we consider the case that NGOs drive climate action in Nigeria and these NGOs are mostly financed from the developed world, it is most improbable that the receiving organisations and states will pursue an agenda different from that of the sponsors. We have explained this vividly in the case of the Nigerian media and the NGOs. Most African countries also suffer this ideological setback. According to Ciplet (2015), during the 2009 UNFCCC meeting in Copenhagen, Ethiopia's president who was Africa's sole representative in the group of countries that were shown the Accord before it was made public contradicted the African Group, Least Developed Countries and Association of Small Island States negotiating blocs. Amidst allegation of promise of humanitarian and military aid for his cooperation, he stood with France and other countries of the developed world in saying that "we have come on almost every issue to a complete understanding of each other's position" (Ciplet, 2015, p.260). In his findings, Ciplet further revealed that the U.S. cut aid of 8.5 million USD to Bolivia and Ecuador for opposing the Copenhagen Accord. An African delegate to the meeting captures it better when he said "the pressure to back the West has been intense… it was done at a very high level and nothing was written down. It was made clear by the EU, UK and France and the US that if they did not back them then they would suffer" (Ciplet, 2015, 260).

But as we lay blame on the hegemonic nature of the UNFCCC as a constraint for developing countries' inability to comply, it is pertinent to credit this international framework for providing leverage for developing countries and their social forces. It should be acknowledged that international regimes also result in gains for these countries. For instance, but for provisions in the UNFCCC for financing adaptation and mitigation in developing countries, very few Non-Annex I or developing countries could afford the cost. The UNFCCC provides avenue for the dominant class to accommodate strategic bottom-up challenges through negotiated interests. What Gramsci calls unstable equilibria of compromise (Ciplet, 2015, p. 257). Somehow, even regime theory of international relations allows for the negotiating of interest. That is the only way the concerns of the developing countries can be heard and considered. After all, some developing countries are also regional powers in their own right. And their behaviour in relation to UNFCCC compliance may also require understanding from that prism.

For countries like Nigeria, South Africa, Egypt and Ethiopia that are also regional powers, this claim may be valid. In the case of Nigeria for instance, her status as a global producer in OPEC should be her overriding interest. It is argued that OPEC as a negotiating bloc in the UN often plays a spoiler's role in climate change negotiations that contradicts the position of the African group. However, Nigeria hardly follows OPEC's position on climate change in spite of the benefits (Bremond, Emmanuel & Mignon, 2012). Moreover, as a developing country, its capacity to abide by any commitment is dependent on assistance from developed countries. But again UNFCCC article 4(h) urges that in the implementing of commitment , full consideration should be given in terms of funding, insurance and technology transfer "to countries whose economies are highly dependent on income generated from the production, processing and export and /or on consumption of fossil fuels and associated energy intensive product". For Nigeria, UNFCCC provides access for promised development that ordinarily cannot be met by domestic resources. In addition, dissociating herself from the convention will threaten her recognition by the developed countries as a regional power against her "manifest destiny on the continent" (Akindele, 1985). Nelson (2016) also amplifies this but with reference to regional powers in Africa. He says, in terms of engagement with climate change politics,

> Not engaging the issue might undermine attempts to demonstrate that the regional power speaks on behalf of the continent in other issue areas. Second, monetary prizes are associated with climate change politics. That is, many of the African priorities involve requests that developed states provide financial assistance and technology transfers to enable adaptation to climate change and to improve the continent's own attempts at mitigation (Nelson, 2016, p.117).

In the case of Nigeria, one can say that her participation in the UNFCCC enhances her leadership role and puts her in a position to determine the directional flow of resources both domestically and on the continent. For these reasons, Nigeria invests efforts to be seen to participate, comply and implement UNFCCC commitments. With a constrained economy and socio-political configuration, Nigeria cannot choose otherwise. It is Nigeria's ultimate desire to be seen as a global valuable partner (Nelson, 2016), but her oil dependent economy limits participation to her full potential. The above goes to show that in a world where economic interests are central to the behaviour of states, the environment and climate change pose serious challenges for economic development.

This therefore calls for new approaches in pursuit of new development. Rudrappan (2011) expresses this better in his treatise that the old development models of development are not carbon neutral and not sustainable. In essence, if states continue pursuing development using the classical models of development, the earth will cease to support life. More carbon related industrial action will lead to increased erosion, global warming, loss of biodiversity and ultimately, loss of balanced income growth and biophysical experience. There is also what he calls the inclusive sustainable globalization theory advocated by Robert Zoellick that stresses Public-Private Partnership for sustainable development which targets poor countries. Unfortunately, like in the case of the neo-classical development models, this model lacks broad-based sustainable growth that acts as antidote for climate risks and vulnerabilities (Rudrappan, 2011). At the end, countries will still contend with vicious cycles of poverty that are synonymous with the classical models. In view of this, developing countries like Nigeria require a sustainable development paradigm that Rudrappan (2011) advocates should create a virtuous cycle of prosperity. This new development agenda focuses on income, social justice and endogenous productivity (Rudrappan, 2011, p.13). It integrates institutional development, technical capacity and diversification of the economy for both domestic and foreign trade with public sector as a strategic partner with the MNC for carbon neutral or green development.

The new development agenda propagated by Rudrappan (2011), comfortably aligns with the needs of developing countries and should determine the direction of global discussions on renewable energy and the green or blue economy. It addresses economic growth, equity, sustainability as well as adaptation and mitigation. This is in stark contrast to the neo-classical model that neglects the environment and so unfit in pursuing climate action under the UNFCCC.

RECOMMENDATIONS

The state of affairs in relation to climate change in Nigeria and the need for intervention by all stakeholders in the climate emergency call for drastic measures. Foremost here is that the UNFCCC's voluntary commitments in the area of adaptation should serve as the guide for ShEs in Nigeria. In doing this, the environmental needs of the affected communities should always be considered. This approach would ensure that climate change initiatives are embraced by the people and can be sustained from generation to generation. Such consideration will facilitate the country's compliance with the UNFCCC and provide a sense of direction to climate action in Nigeria. Climate change adaptation should also be given priority attention in government's climate action. It is adaptation that can protect the people and build their resilience to the devastating impact of climate change. In this regard, the public sector must seek more partners and NGOs that promote adaptation to protect livelihood and the ecosystem. This may involve reaching beyond European partners and NGOs to other continents where adaptation measures are considered central to climate action.

In order for Nigeria to fully comply with her commitments under the UNFCCC, the public sector must also open up the space for conversation and investment in climate action by providing the enabling environment for clean energy entrepreneurs to thrive both in terms of mitigation and adaptation. The active participation of the private sector is central in the development of capacity for adaptation and mitigation, bearing in mind the new global emphasis on the green economy which has emerged as the new development agenda. In this light, the Nigerian public sector as the chief custodian of the UNFCCC in the country must encourage more actors to participate in climate action. Encouraging and enabling more social forces to coordinate climate action will go a long way in creating the enabling environment for both adaptation and mitigation to occur. The fact that climate change is an anthropogenic activity calls for more engagement of the private sector, the media, community leaders, youth groups and researches in the academia. Aid should be complemented with entrepreneurship for sustainable results. It is also expedient on Nigeria to engage developed countries more aggressively in order to receive assistance as provided in the UNFCCC. The present scenario where the country passively waits on the developed countries to seize the initiatives to build Nigeria's capacity will not yield timely result in terms of climate action or capacity building.

There's also need for strong political will on the part of public sector at all levels to commit to climate action. Without the right political will from public sector, there's a limit to what any individual or group can achieve in terms of climate action or compliance with the UNFCCC. Public sector's focus should shift from merely satisfying immediate or expedient socio-economic goals to the pursuit of sustainable development. There's need to harmonise public sector's development plans and sustainable development. This calls for better coordination of Nigeria's environmental agencies with a view to strategically attend to Nigeria's environmental needs which are further impacted by climate change and affect the country's ability to comply with her UNFCCC commitments most especially adaptation. Radical approaches like inter-agency cooperation will definitely address the country's environmental needs which are impacted by multifaceted factors that require strategy to solve. The desire here is for deliberate policies with timelines on the shift from fossil-based production to an economy and production that is carbon neutral.

THE FINAL WORD

We have seen the extent to which Nigeria as an oil producing country complied with her UNFCCC obligations. Principally, the Kyoto Protocol under the UNFCCC identifies six gases as the principal causes of global warming resulting in climate change and calls for actions to reduce the emission of these gases. These are carbondioxide, methane, nitrous oxide, hydrofluorocarbon, perfluorocarbon, sulphur hexafluoride including nitrogen trifluoride and hydrofluorinated ethers. The document enjoins all countries to adopt mitigation and adaptation measures to face climate change. Mitigation entails preventing the emission of these gases. In terms of adaptation, the UNFCCC calls on states, most especially developing countries to take actions to adjust to the effects of global warming like storms and changes in weather patterns. Thus mitigation and adaptation action constitute compliance under the UNFCCC. We also established that Nigeria's participation in the UNFCCC is constrained by the structural nature of power in the international system which is framed and designed to serve the interest of powerful states in the world. Even the UNFCCC reflects this structure. Thus, it is only with the support of the powerful developed countries that Nigeria can comply with her UNFCCC commitments.

We see in the preceding chapters that Nigeria has not significantly complied with her UNFCCC commitments. Poor political will, weak capacity, inadequate finance, poor policy formulation and implementation were identified among the reasons for Nigeria's lukewarm compliance record. In the analyses, we see that critical to Nigeria's compliance, is the need for action in the area of adaptation which is the focus for developing countries under the UNFCCC. We also see that public sector and NGOs are the main influencers of climate action in Nigeria amidst other social forces like media, community leaders, academics, organized private sector. Going forward, more publicity, most especially by the media and capacity building in terms of monitoring, reporting and verification will be necessary. The advice from local experts is that adaptation is less expensive, less complicated and saves more lives in communities that are vulnerable to climate change. Adaptation is also more amenable to Nigeria's environmental need of erosion, desertification, land and air pollution, flood, waste management and land degradation which require environmental protection measures.

In the light of these, there is urgent need to address capacity in adaptation beginning with less costly measures. The priority should be adaptation and its impact on livelihood. Mitigation comes after, bearing in mind its long-term economic and development advantages for Nigeria. The lessons in this text are not only applicable to Nigeria. They are useful to every developing country in the face of the current precarious climate emergency.

POSTSCRIPT

Whilst this book was under production, Nigeria released its Third National Communication to the UNFCCC. With my focus on the book, I was unable to fully peruse Nigeria's TNC, but from face value, it contained broad climate action initiatives. The government's rising use of solar power in rural electrification is quite remarkable. Certainly, the country deserves commendation for her efforts to follow through with these climate actions against many odds.

Going forward, I will like to challenge local scholars in climate governance to build on the foundation of this book. There's need for additional literature to expand the frontiers of research in specific areas. More animated inquiry on the Role of Developed Countries in Nigeria's Climate Change Actions will significantly transform the scientific and social traction of the subject at home. And given the looming climate emergency, I believe that further studies in the following areas will also be instructive both now and in the future:

  i. Assessment of Adaptation Mechanisms of the UNFCCC and its Impact and Implications for Developing Countries.
  ii. Developing Countries and Mitigation under the UNFCCC: An Assessment of Options for Nigeria.
  iii. Climate Change as the New Foreign Policy Agenda: A Critique of Climate Change Negotiations at Conference of Parties (COP) Meetings.

In addition, having dwelt on Nigeria as a single unit in this literature, the next phase is to concentrate on specific areas domestically. This suggestion takes cognisance that environmental issues which include climate action fall under the constitution's concurrent legislative list. Hence, this calls for further investigations that dwell on the granular data of climate governance in particular areas. In this light, intensive studies on each of the geographical/environmental zones in the country with regards to the nature of climate change and climate action as well as key stakeholders involved, will greatly enhance the coordination of climate governance in the country. For instance, it will be informative to investigate the nature of climate governance in "upper northern" Nigeria with its Sahelian-Savannah landscape. A corpus on the challenges in the desiccating lake chad region and the stakeholders driving the process will also be ground-breaking. Similar argument can be adduced for the mangrove rainforest in the south of Nigeria. Thus, an exposé indicating the principal drivers of climate action in these regions, especially, government's interventions will greatly advance climate governance and Nigeria's compliance with her international commitments. It will equally be edifying to collate domestic climate actions that are not strictly undertaken as a response to any international mandate. Here I mean climate action by non-state actors. Rigorous interrogations of all these concerns are central to Nigeria's deep decarbonisation pathways in the foreseeable future.

In essence, by providing this overview, I have set the ball rolling for others to dig deeper. This publication is therefore a precursor to more robust studies on climate governance in Nigeria. After all, the campaigns for more effective climate governance in the country call for more intense studies focusing on specific issues and the dynamics involved. I believe that heeding this advice in the long run, will eventually activate the country's climate governance from its current lethargy. With this momentum, Nigeria could closely follow countries that are already set to transit to complete carbon neutrality in the mid-decades of the 21st century.

REFERENCES

Abimbola, A. (2002). Pressure Groups and the Democratic Process in Nigeria (1979-1993). *Nordic Journal of African studies*, 11 (1), 38-47.

Adache, J. (2013). Africa and the Challenge of Climate Change. African Strategic Review, 3(1 & 2) Jan-Dec 2013.

Africa Development Bank (2014). AfDB Action Plan on Climate Change. http//: www.afdb.org

Ahmadu, A. (2015), Think Tanks and Foreign Policy: The Nigerian Experience. A Salon Seminar Presentation at the Study of the United States Institute on U.S. Foreign Policy at Bard College, Annandale-On-Hudson. New York. July 23, 2015

Ajao, R. & Ogunniyi, E. (2009). Nigeria and Climate Change: Road to Cop15, Abuja: Federal Ministry of Environment.

Akindele, R. (1985). *The Organization and Promotion of World Peace: A Study of Universal-Regional Relationships.* Toronto: University of Toronto Press.

Amadi, A. (2008). Social, Political and Economic Perspectives of Air Pollution Control in Nigeria, In: A. Amadi (Ed.) Proceedings of The National Seminar on Air Pollution and Industrialization in Nigeria. Lagos: Community Conservation and Development Initiatives (CCDI Ecology and Development Series 1), 9–15

Amaza, I. (2018). The Nigeria Gas Flare Commercialisation Programme: A Win-Win Situation? www.mondaq.com

Amsden, A. (2003). The Rise of the Rest, Challenges to the West from Late-Industrializing Economies, New York: Oxford University Press.

Annandale D, David A, Daniela C, María E, John H, Joseph M, Peter M, Jyotsna P, Giang P, and Andreas R (2019). Independent evaluation of the Green Climate Fund's Environmental and Social Safeguards and the Environmental and Social Management System. Benchmarking study, July 2019. https://ieu.greenclimate.fund/documents

Anwadike, C. (2017). Kyoto Protocol and the Challenges of Implementation in Nigeria. Journal of Geography, Environment & Earth Science International. Vol. 13 Issue 1.

Ati, O., Agubamah, E., & Abaje, I. (2018). Global Climate Change Policies and Politics: Nigeria's Response. FUDMA Journal of Politics and International Affairs. Vol. No. 1 Dec. 2018.

Atkinson, H. (2013). Politics of Climate Change: Meeting the Challenge and Making of Change. Political Insight Vol. 4 Issue 2. Sept. 2013, 230-33

Batta, H., Ashong, A. & Bashir, S. (2013). Press Coverage of Climate Change Issues in Nigeria and Implications for Public Participation Opportunities. Journal of Sustainable Development, 6(2).

Bhullar, L. (2013). REDD+ And the Clean Development Mechanism: A Comparative Perspective. International Journal of Rural Law and Policy. 2013 Special Edition. https://epress.lib.uts.edu.au/journals/index.

Bob, C. (2001). Marketing Rebellion: Insurgent Groups, International media, and NGO support. International Politics. 38, 311-334

Bob, C. (2002). Globalization and the Social Construction of Human Rights Campaigns. In: A.Brysk, ed., Globalization and Human Rights. [online] Berkeley: University of California Press, pp.133-147. Available at: https://www.dawsonera.com/readonline/9780520936287

Bremond, V., Emmanuel, H. & Mignon, V. (2012). Does OPEC Still Exist as A Cartel? An Empirical Investigation. Energy Economics 34 (1). 125-131

Carter, N. (2007). The Politics of the Environment: Ideas, Activism, Policy, Cambridge: Cambridge University Press, 2nd edition (1st edition 2001).

CCC. (2016). Carbon Budgets and targets. https://www.theccc.org.uk/tackling-climate change/reducing-carbon-emissions/carbon-budgets-and-targets/

Chang, H.J. (2009). Hamlet without Prince of Denmark: How Development Has Disappeared from Today's 'Development' Discourse, In Sharukh Rafi Khan & Jens Christiansen (eds.) *Towards New developmentalism: Market as means rather than as master* (47-58).

Chayes, A., & Antonia, C. (1995). *The New Sovereignty: Compliance with International Agreements.* Cambridge, MA: Harvard University Press.

REFERENCES

Ciplet, D. (2015). Rethinking Cooperation: Inequality and Consent in International Climate Change Politics. Global Governance 21, 247-274.

Cochran, W (1977). Sampling Techniques. New York: John and Wiley Pub.

Connor, R. & Dovers, S. (2004). Institutional Change for Sustainable Development. Journal of Environmental Law. Vol. 17. Issue. 3

Dada, F. O. A., Jibrin, G. M., & Ze Ijeoma, A. (2006). *Secondary Atlas*. Ibadan: Macmillan. Nigeria.

Davoudi, S., Crawford H., & Mehmood, A. (2009). *Planning for Climate Change: Strategies for Mitigation and Adaptation.* London: Earthscan.

Dauvergne, P. (2004). *Handbook of Global Environmental Politics*. Cheltenham: Edward Elgar Publishing Limited.

Dilling, L., & Berggren, J. (2014). What Do Stakeholders Need to Manage for Climate Change and Variability? A Document-Based Analysis from Three Mountain States in the Western USA. https://www.researchgate.net/publication/271504220

Dilonardo, M. (2019). Why Africa is Building a Great Green Wall. www.mnn.com

Easterling, W. (1999). Adapting Agriculture to Climate Change. Oxford: Clarendon Press.

EC. (2015), www.ec.europa.eu/china/policies/adaptation/ir www.sciencepolicy. colorado.edu/ admin

Elenwo, E. & Akankali, J. (2003). Environmental Policies and Strategies in Nigeria Oil and Gas Industry: Gains, Challenges and Prospects. http://www.scirp.org/journal/nr

EPA (2014). Climate Change Mitigation: EPA's Role in President Obama's Action Plan. www.epa.gov.usa

Fairchild (1976). Chapter 14. In: Rummel. R. The Conflict Helix.

Fairchild, H. Ed. (1970). Dictionary of Sociology and Related Sciences. New Jersey: Littlefield, Adams.

Falaki, A. & Adegbija, V. (2013). Investigating the Use of the Media in Disseminating Information on Climate Change in North Central Nigeria. Global Media Journal African Edition, 2013 7(1),13-39

Falkner, R. (2004) *A Minilateral Solution for Global Climate Change? On Bargaining Efficacy, Club Benefits and International Legitimacy.* Working Paper No. 197. Grant Research Institute on Climate Change and the Environment London.

FMEnv (Federal Ministry of Environment Housing and Urban Development) (2003). Nigeria's First National Communication under the United Nations Framework Convention on Climate Change, Abuja.

Federal Ministry of Environment, (2018). Climate Change Stakeholders Meeting on Intended Nationally Determined Contribution held in Lagos on 2 July 2018.

FMI. (2016). *The Evolution of Nigeria.* www.fmi.gov.ng/about-nigeria/history. First National Communication. (2003). Federal Ministry of Environment Abuja.

Ford, J. & Berrang-Ford, L. (2011). Systematic Review of Observed Climate Change Adaptation. https://link.springer.com/Article/10.1007/S10584-011-0045-

Gichira, P., Agwata, J. & Muigua, K. (2014). Climate finance: Fears and Hopes for Developing Countries. Journal of Law, Policy and Globalisation. 22

Giddens, A. (2008). *The Politics of Climate Change: National Responses to the Challenge of Global Warming.* www.Policy-Network.Net

Giddens, A. (2011). *The Politics of Climate Change.* London: Polity Press.

Global Commission on the Economy and Climate (2018). www.premiumtimesng.com

Goldblatt, M. & Middleton, J. (2007). Climate policy Coherence and Institutional Coordination: Clarifying Institutional Responsibilities in South Africa (Basic 13)

Government of Canada (2016). Canada Way Forward on Climate Change. www.climatechange. gc.ca/default

Goving, S., Selvi, T. & Karuppaiah, P (2017). Climate Smart Agriculture. https://www.slideshare.net/tmthatchupeacefeul/climate-smart-agriculture-74290266

Gupta, J. (2008). Engaging Developing Countries in Climate Change Negotiations. Policy Note PE 401.007 European Parliament.

Guzman, A. (2008). How International Law Works: A Rational Choice Theory. New York: Oxford University Press

REFERENCES

Habib, B. (2011). Climate Change and the International Relations Theory: Northeast Asia as a Case Study. *Third Global International Studies Conference*, Porto, Portugal: University of Porto, Portugal, (2011), p. 14. Accessed on February 20, 2014. http://www.wiscnetwork.org/porto2011/papers/WISC_2011-562.pdf.

Happer, C & Philoa, G. (2013). *The Role of the Media in the Construction of Public Belief and Social Change.* Journal of Social and Political Psychology, vol. 1 no. 1. pp 78-90.

Hay, C. (2001). *What Place for Ideas in the Structure-Agency Debate? Globalisation as a Process without a Subject.* http://www.criticalrealism.com/archive/cshay_wpisad.html.

Hefron, D. (2015). *What Do Realist Think About Climate Change?* Working Paper for the Centre for Geopolitics and Security in Realism Studies, London.

Henry Boll Foundation (2018). Policy Research on the Imposition of 10% tariff Duties on Solar Components: Making a Way for Solar in Nigeria. Abuja: Centre for Social Justice

House, F. (1925). The Concept of Social Forces in American Sociology. *American Journal of Sociology.* 31, 145-156

Hussein, A. & Karaye, U. (2015). The Anticipated Socio-Economic Impact of Climate Change in Nigeria. Paper Presentation at the 29th Annual General Meeting of the Nigeria Meteorological Association in Sokoto.

Hussey, J. & Hussey, R. (1997). Business Research. Basingstoke: Macmillan Press.

ICEED (2019). Nigeria Adopts Climate Change Policy Document. http//: www.iceednigeria.org

Ibitoye, F. & Akinbami, J. (1999). Strategies for implementation of CO2-mitigation options in Nigeria's energy sector. Applied Energy Journal, Volume 63, Issue 1, May 1999, Pages 1-16.

Isabel, O. & Esther A. (2009). Personal correspondence on FMEnv on COPs 22.

IPCC (2010). *Understanding Climate Change: 22 years of IPCC Assessment Intergovernmental Panel on Climate Change.* www.ipcc.int.gov

Jacobson, H. & Weiss, E. (1998). Engaging Countries-Strengthening compliance with International Environmental Accord. MIT Press

Kalejaiye, P. & Aliyu, N. (2013). Ethnic Politics and Social Conflicts: Factors in Nigeria's Underdevelopment. Journal of International Social Research 27 Volume, 6 Issue, 45-54

Keck, M. & Skink, K. (1998). *Activists Beyond Borders: Advocacy Networks in International Politics.* Cornell: University Press Ithaca.

Keeling C., & Whorf T. (1994). Atmospheric CO2 Records from the Sites in the SIO Air Sampling Network http://journals.sagepub.com/doi/abs/10.1177/2053019613516289

Koblowsky, P & Speranza C.I. (2010). Institutional challenges to developing a Nigerian climate policy. Paper at the Berlin Conference on the human dimensions of global environmental change: Social dimensions of environmental change and governance.

Koh, H. (1998). Why Do Nations Obey International Law? Houston International law review. 623

Kratochwill J., & Ruggie, G. (1986). International Organization: A state of the Art. *International Organization* 40, 753-775.

Kuuispalo, R. (2017). Exiled by Emissions: Climate Change Related Displacement and Migration in International Law: Gaps in Global Governance and the Role of the UN Climate Convention. Vermont Journal of Environmental Law. Vol. 18 Issue 4, 614-647.

Kythreotis, A. (2012). Progress in Global Climate Change Policy? Reasserting National State Territoriality in A 'Post-Political' World. Sage Journal 36(4), 457-474.

Mendelsohn, R & Dinar, A. (1999). Climate Change Agriculture and Developing Countries Nations: Does Adaptation Matter? World Bank Research Observer Vol. 14 pp.277-293

Mersha, G. (2009) International Agricultural Land Deals Awards Ethiopian Virgin Lands to Foreign Companies. http//www.farmlandgrab.org

Middlehurst, C. (2017). China dominates top 200 clean tech companies list. China Dialogue February 22. http//www.chinadialogue.net

Michael, M. & Stephen, S. (2008). Global Warming. Washington: Encarta Microsoft Corp.

Midgal, J., Kohli, A. & Shue, V. (1994). *State Power and Social Forces: Domination and Transformation in the Third World.* Cambridge: Cambridge University Press.

REFERENCES

Morgenthau, H. (1952). Another Great Debate: The National Interest of the United States. *American Political Science Review* 46 (4), 961-962.

Muhammad, A., Shagari, N. & Gatawa, B. (2012). Climate Change in Nigeria: Adaptation and Mitigation Strategies in the 21st Century. Paper presented at the 29th Annual General Meeting of the Nigerian Meteorological Society 23-26 November 2012).

Mustapha, M, Yunusa, A & Mukhtari, A. (2015). A Review of Climate Change Mitigation and Adaptation Strategies Towards Sustainable Development. Proceedings of 52 Annual Conference of Association of Nigerian Geographers.

Nandy, P. (2017). What is the Significance of the Paris Agreement? Renewal Journal, 24(1), 47-52

NASA. (2011). What's in a Name? Global Warming vs. Climate Change. http://www. nasa.gov/topics/earth/features/climate_by_any_other_name.html

Nebo, C. O (2015). Press Release by the Honourable Minister of Power. Federal Ministry of Power.

Nelson, M. (2016). Africa's Regional Powers and Climate Change Negotiations. Global Environmental Politics. 16(2) May 2016. MIT Press.

Ngoweh, I.W. (2016). Compliance with Multilateral Environmental Agreements (MEAs): The Case Of Cameroon and the United Nations Framework Convention on Climate Change (UNFCCC) and Its Kyoto Protocol. Thesis for the award of Master of International Relations, International Relations Institute of Cameroon (IRIC).

Nkeki, F., Henah, P. & Nduka O. (2013). Geospatial Techniques for the Assessment and Analysis of Flood Risk along the Niger-Benue Basin in Nigeria. Journal of Geographic Information System Vol.5 No.2(2013). https://www.scirp. org/html/3-8401214_29778.htm.

Nnaji, C. (2009). Climate Change and Socio-Economic Development in Nigeria. *Paper Presented at a Conference on Climate Change and the Nigerian Environment Organized by the Department of Geography University of Nigeria, Nsukka, Between June 29th and July 2nd.*

Nnoli, O. (1978). Ethnic Politics in Nigeria, Enugu: Fourth Dimension Publishers.

Nnimmo, B. (2015). Nigeria's Climate and Environmental Crisis. Paper Presented at Shehu Musa Yar Adua Centre, Abuja.

NNPC. (2015). Nigeria Unveils New Climate Policy.http://www.nnpcgroup.com/ Public Relations/NNPCinthenews/tabid/9

Nwabueze, C. (2007). Environmental Communication: Perspectives on Green Communication and Information Management Enugu: Daisy Press.

Obi, C. (2003). Political and social dimensions of environmental crisis in Nigeria, in: Darkoh, M & Rwomire, R. (eds.): Human impact on environment and sustainable development in Africa, Aldershot, Burlington: Ashgate (Contemporary Perspectives on Developing Societies, 43–53

Ogbodo, G. & Stewart, N. (2014). Climate Change and Nigeria's Sustainable Development of Vision 20-2020. Annual Survey of International and Comparative Law 20 (1), 1-34.

Okeke, D. C. (2004). Government efforts in environmental management in Nigeria, in: H. C. Mba et al. (eds.): Management of environmental problems and hazards in Nigeria, Aldershot, Burlington: Ashgate, 189–203

Okorodudu-Fubara, M. (2001). Refocusing Regulatory Regime on Atmospheric Pollution Control. In: Osuntokun, A. (Ed.) (2002). Democracy and Sustainable Development in Nigeria, Lagos: Friedrich Stiftung.

Oladipo, E. (2010). Towards Enhancing the Adaptive Capacity of Nigeria: A Review of the Country's State of Preparedness for Climate Change Adaptation. A Report Submitted to The Henry Boll Foundation Nigeria.

Olawuyi, D. (2017). From Technology Transfer to Technology Absorption: Addressing Climate Technology Gaps in Africa. Fixing Governance Paper Series No. 5, June 2017.

Oludoro, O. (2015). Mitigating the Effects of Climate Change in Sub-Saharan Africa Via an Effective International Legal Standard: A Case Study of Nigeria. Doctoral Thesis, Faculty of Law, University of Ghent, Netherland.

Onafeso, D., Cornelius, A. & Adegbayi, H. (2017). Appraisal of Climate Change Adaptation in Nigeria.

Onyema, E. (2005). Economic Diplomacy & Conduct of Nigeria's External Relations: Analysis of the National Economic Empowerment Strategy (NEEDS). Dissertation for the Award of PhD Political Science, University of Nigeria Nsukka.

Opara, C. & Yerima, B. (2014). The Impact Of Climate Change on Sub-Saharan Africa : Case Studies in Cameroon, Nigeria and Uganda. Frankfurt: Peterlang Pub.

Osha, S. (2006). Birth of the Ogoni Protest Movement. Journal of Asian and African Studies,41(1-2), pp.13-38.

Paradi, M., Stefan, H., Tabare, C. & Richard, Y. (2014). The Global Cleantedh Innovation Index 2014: Nurturing Tomorrow's Transofrmative Entrepreneurs. http//www.report_gkivak_ckeabtecg_ubbivatuib_ubdex_2014

Park, R. & Burgess, E (2009). Introduction to the Science of Sociology. Release online by the Gutenberg project. https://www.gutenberg.net

Parry, M., Canzian, O., Palutiko, F., Van Der Linden, P., Pau, J., & Hansen, G. (eds). (2007). Climate Change Impact, Adaptation and Vulnerability. Cambridge: Cambridge University Press.

Perry J. (1976). The Social Web: An Introduction to Sociology. Second Edition. New York: Harper & Row Publishers.

Pherm, J. (2008). What is in the National Interest? Hans Morgenthau's Realist Vision and American Foreign Policy. *American Foreign Policy Interest Journal* 30, 256-265.

Pielke, R. (2009). Global Warming. In Enclyclopedia Britannica. Chicago: Encyclopaedia Britannica.

Rayner, T. & Okereke, C. (2007). The Politics of Climate Change, In: C. Okereke (Ed.): The Politics of the Environment: A Survey. London: Routledge, 116–135

Rhodes, R. (1997). Understanding Governance. Milton Keynes: Open University Press.

Rudrappan, D. (2011). Reconciling Climate Change and Economic Growth: The Need for an Alternative Paradigm of Development. Covenant University 34 Public Lecture Series.

Rummel, R.J. (1976). Chapter 14. Understanding Conflict and War: The Conflict Helix Vol. 2. California: Sage Publications.

Sani, M. (2018). Understanding the Concept of the Great Green Wall Initiative. Leadership Newspaper, July 10, 2018

Schenkel, W. (2000). From Clean Air to Climate Policy in The Netherlands And Switzerland: How Two States Deal with A Global Problem, Swiss Political Science Review 6 (1)

Scott, J. (2016). External and Internal Pressures on Radical Social Movements: Tracing the (De)Mobilization of the League of Revolutionary Black Workers. Thesis for the Award of Master of Arts, DePaul University Chicago, Illinois.

Sharna, J. (2016). Pocket Guide to Capacity Building for Climate Change. Bonn: European Centre for Building Institutions.

Soroos, M. (2011), *Global Institutions and the Environment.* Washington DC: CQ Press.

Spaliviero, M. Dapper, M. & Maló, S. (2014). Flood Analysis of the Limpopo River Basin through Past Evolution, Reconstruction and Geomorphological Approach. https://www.researchgate.net/publication/307837393

Tarfa, P. (2017). Combatting Climate Change and Creating Opportunities through Technology Innovation. Paper Presented At the 13the International Conference of The Nigeria Computer Society

Teichman, J. (2012). Social Forces and States: Poverty and Distributional Outcomes in South Korea, Chile, and Mexico. Stanford: University Press.

Thisday Newspaper, November 27, 2018. Okereke: Climate Change May Cost Nigeria $460bn by 2050

Tope, O (2011). Nigerian Peacekeeping Mission Under The Auspices Of The Un Security Council From 1960 To 2010: A Study Of Sierra Leone. https://www.omotere.tk

Ukonu, M., Akpan, C. & Anorue, L. (2012). Nigerian Newspaper Coverage of Climate Change (2009-2010). New Media and Mass Communication Vol. 5. No. 12

UNDP (United Nations Development Programme) (2008). Human Development Report 2007/2008: Fighting Climate Change: Human Solidarity in A Divided World, Nairobi: UNDP; online: http://hdr.undp.org/en/media/HDR_20072008_EN_Complete.pdf

UNDP Annual Report (2015). UNDP Nigeria. www.undp –annual-report.org

UNECA, (2010). A Technology Transfer for Africa's Development.http//www.repository. uneca.org/handle

UNEP. (2001). *International Environmental Governance: Multilateral Environmental Agreements.* doc. UNEP/IGM/1/INF (6 April 2001), para.4.

REFERENCES

UNEP. (2006). Manual on Compliance with and Enforcement of Multilateral Environmental Agreement.

UNFCCC (1994) United Nations Framework Convention on Climate Change. https://unfccc.int/Resource/Docs/Convkp/Conveng.pdf

UNFCCC (2003). Caring for the Climate: a guide to the climate change convention and protocol. UNFCCC secretariat Bonn. Germany

UNFCCC (2004). *First Ten Years*. https://unfccc.int/resource/docs/publications/first_ten_years _en.pdf

UNFCCC (2005). Sixth Compilation and Synthesis of Initial National Communications from Parties Not Included in Annex I To the Convention. http://unfccc.int/2860.php

UNFCCC. (2014). *The United Nation Framework Convention on Climate Change.* http://unfccc. int/2860.php

US National Research Council (2010). Advancing the Science of Climate Change; America's Climate Choices: Panel on Advancing the Science of Climate Change. Washington, D.C. The National Academies Press.

Vanguard (2018). Osinbajo Wants Local Technologies to Deal with Climate Change Issues. Vanguard Newspaper 4 August 2018.

Vogler, J. (2016). Climate Change in World Politics. London: Palmgrave Macmillan.

Voigt, C. (2016). The Compliance and Implementation Mechanism of the Paris Agreement. Review of European Community and International Environmental Law. Vol. 25 No. 2.

Wang, X., & Wiser, G. (2002). The Implementation and Compliance Regimes Under the Change Convention and Its Kyoto Protocol. Oxford: Blackwell Publishers.

Wagner, A. (2003). *The Foreign Policies of the Global South: Rethinking Conceptual Frameworks.* Colorado: Lynne Rienner Publishers.

WESP (2014), Country Classification by World Economic Situation and Prospects of the UN.https://www.un.org/en/development/desa/policy/wesp/wesp_current/2014wesp_country_classification.pdf

World Bank, (2010). Rising Global Interest in Farmlands: Can It Yield Sustainable and Equitable Benefits? http//www.siteresources.worldbank.org

World Bank, (2015). Little Green Data Book. www.worldbank.org

World Bank, (2016). New Data Reveals Uptick in Global Gas Flaring. www. worldbank.org

World Summit on Sustainable Development (WSSD) (2002). The Johannesburg Declaration. http://www.un-documents.net

ZinnKann, J. (2014). Capacity Building and Awareness raising on climate change adaptation in the private sector. www. Adelphi.de.en/project.

Zirra, Z., Usman T. & Modibbo, A.S. (2019). *Non-Governmental Organisations and Climate Change Action in Nigeria.* International Journal of Current Innovations in Academic Research. Vol. 2 Issue 7 pp. 67-74.

Zirra, Z., Usman, T. & Modibbo, S. (2019). *The Utility of Mixed Methodology for Climate Governance Research in Nigeria.* International Journal of Current Innovations in Academic Research. Vol. 3 Issue 4 & pp. 163-170.

Zirra, Z. (2019). Assessment of Nigeria's Compliance with the UNFCCC. Doctoral Thesis in International Relations. Department of Political Science, Nasarawa State University, Keffi. Nigeria.

..............1999 Constitution of the Federal Republic of Nigeria. Lagos: Federal Government Press.

.............."Nigeria". Encyclopaedia Brittanica. https://www.britannica.com/place/ Nigeria.

..............Nigeria's Intended Nationally Determined Contributions (INDCs) (2016) Prepared by the Federal Ministry of Environment, Abuja, Nigeria. Available at https//www.climatelinks.org.

..............The United Nations Framework Convention on Climate Change (21 March 1994).

APPENDIX A
RESEARCH QUESTIONNAIRE

SECTION A - Profile

Sector: _____Public   _____Private   _____NGO

Gender: _____Male   _____Female

Highest Educational Qualifications:

      _____O Level   _____Degree/HND

      _____Post-Graduate   _____Professional

Experience in Climate Change Policy Action:

      _____1-5 Yrs   _____6-10 Yrs   _____Above 10 Yrs

SECTION B - Questions
Theme: Nigeria's Environmental Needs

1. *Do you agree that Nigeria's UNFCCC commitments are affected by her environmental needs?*

    ○ Strongly Agree
    ○ Agree
    ○ Undecided
    ○ Disagree
    ○ Strongly Disagree

2. *Can you mention Nigeria's environmental needs?*

    . . . .
    . . . .
    . . . .
    . . . .
    . . . .

3. *Do you agree that Nigeria's environmental needs drive her ability to comply with the UNFCCC Commitments?*

   ○ Strongly agree
   ○ Agree
   ○ Undecided
   ○ Disagree
   ○ Strongly Disagree

Theme: Social Forces

4. *To what extent is Nigeria's compliance with the UNFCCC Commitments driven by social forces.*

   ○ Large Extent
   ○ Some Extent
   ○ Undecided
   ○ Small Extent
   ○ No Extent

5. *Can you mention the social forces that drive climate change action in Nigeria?*

   . . . .
   . . . .
   . . . .
   . . . .
   . . . .

6. *Can you explain how social forces drive Nigeria's compliance with the UNFCCC Commitments?*

   . . . .
   . . . .
   . . . .
   . . . .
   . . . .

Theme: Climate Change Compliance Action

7. *In the last ten years, how would you rate Nigeria's Mitigation Action in compliance with the UNFCCC?*

   ○ Very Good
   ○ Good
   ○ Average
   ○ Bad
   ○ Very Bad

8. *In the last ten years, how would you rate Nigeria's Adaptation Action in compliance with the UNFCCC?*

   ○ Very Good
   ○ Good
   ○ Average
   ○ Bad
   ○ Very Bad

9. *In the last ten years, how would you rate the efforts of the private sector in driving climate change action in Nigeria?*

   ○ Very Good
   ○ Good
   ○ Average
   ○ Bad
   ○ Very Bad

INSIGHTS ON DOMESTIC STAKEHOLDERS AND CLIMATE ACTION

10. *In the last ten years, how would you rate the efforts of NGOs/CSOs in driving climate change action in Nigeria?*

    ○ Very Good
    ○ Good
    ○ Average
    ○ Bad
    ○ Very Bad

11. *In the last ten years, how would you rate the efforts of government in driving climate change action in Nigeria?*

    ○ Very Good
    ○ Good
    ○ Average
    ○ Bad
    ○ Very Bad

12. *In the last ten years, how would you rate the efforts of developed countries in driving climate change action in Nigeria?*

    ○ Very Good
    ○ Good
    ○ Average
    ○ Bad
    ○ Very Bad

13. *Do you agree that Nigeria has complied with the UNFCCC agreement in the last ten years?*

      ○ Strongly agree
      ○ Agree
      ○ Undecided
      ○ Disagree
      ○ Strongly Disagree

14. *What are Nigeria's challenges in complying with the UNFCCC? Explain*

. . . .
. . . .
. . . .
. . . .
. . . .

15. *What are your suggestion to enable Nigeria comply with the UNFCCC commitments?*

. . . .
. . . .
. . . .
. . . .
. . . .

APPENDIX B
INTERVIEW SCHEDULE

SECTION A - Profile

Sector: _____Public   _____Private   _____NGO

Gender: _____Male   _____Female

Highest Educational Qualifications:

       _____O Level   _____Degree/HND

       _____Post-Graduate   _____Professional

Experience in Climate Change Policy Action:

       _____1-5 Yrs   _____6-10 Yrs   _____Above 10 Yrs

SECTION B - Interview

1. *Are you aware of Nigeria's commitments under the UNFCCC?*

    a. What is the nature of Nigeria's commitments under the UNFCCC?
    b. Do you think Nigeria's commitments under the UNFCCC address her environmental needs?
    c. What constitutes Nigeria's environmental needs?
    d. Do you think Nigeria's environmental needs drive her ability to comply with the UNFCCC?
    e. How has Nigeria complied with the UNFCCC?

2. *Do you think Social forces/actors play a role in Nigeria's climate change actions?*

   a. What social forces/actors drive Nigeria's compliance with the UNFCCC?
   b. How do social forces/actors facilitate Nigeria's compliance with the UNFCCC?
   c. How do social forces/actors impede Nigeria's compliance with the UNFCCC?
   d. In the last ten years do you think the private sector has significantly driven climate change action in Nigeria?
   e. In the last ten years do you think NGOs have significantly driven climate change action in Nigeria?
   f. In the last ten years do you think Government has significantly driven climate change action in Nigeria?

3. *Do you think Nigeria has complied with her UNFCCC commitments?*

   a. How has Nigeria complied with her UNFCCC Agreement in terms of adaptation?
   b. How has Nigeria complied with her UNFCCC Agreement in terms of mitigation?

4. *Can Nigeria improve her compliance with the UNFCCC Agreement?*

   a. What are your suggestions on how Nigeria can comply with the UNFCCC Agreement?
   b. What are your suggestions on how Nigeria can be assisted internationally to comply with the UNFCCC Agreement?

ABOUT THE AUTHOR

ZAKARI ZIRRA is a multilateral expert from Nigeria and has worked in Africa, Europe and North America. Originally from Bazza, north-east Nigeria, he holds Bachelor's, Master's and Doctorate degrees from the University of Ibadan, University of Maiduguri and the Nasarawa State University respectively. His foreign policy expertise is with emphasis on climate governance in developing countries, as well as carbon assessment of corporate organisations. He is an active member of the Association of Foreign Relations Professionals of Nigeria and the Association of Climate Change Officers. Previously he was a university teacher and has published articles in peer-reviewed journals and book chapters.

www.ingramcontent.com/pod-product-compliance
Lightning Source LLC
Chambersburg PA
CBHW051427090426
42737CB00014B/2859